Multiple Approaches to the Study of

India's Early Past

Multiple Approaches to the Study of India's Early Past

Essays in Theoretical Archaeology

K. Paddayya, FSA
Emeritus Professor and Former Director,
Deccan College (Deemed University), Pune

Aryan Books International
New Delhi

Multiple Approaches to the Study of India's Early Past:
Essays in Theoretical Archaeology

ISBN: 978-81-7305-478-5

Published in **2014** by
Aryan Books International
Pooja Apartments, 4B, Ansari Road, New Delhi-110 002 (India)
Tel.: 23287589, 23255799; Fax: 91-11-23270385
E-mail: aryanbooks@gmail.com
www.aryanbooks.co.in

Designed and Printed in India by
ABI Prints & Publishing Co., New Delhi

Dedicated to the Memory of

Bendapudi Subbarao

(1923-1962)

&

Lewis Roberts Binford

(1931-2011)

Preface

The most striking development that the discipline of archaeology witnessed during the last half-century concerns neither the discovery of any spectacular new site nor any awe-inspiring finding. Instead, it deals with the growth of intense theoretical stirrings. The emergence of the New Archaeology in the 1960s and, later, the rise of ideational or interpretive archaeology have truly lowered the epistemological foundations of the discipline by offering an array of fresh theoretical perspectives for reading the meanings of man's works and products across time and space.

India is one of the few regions outside the Anglo-American world which almost immediately responded positively to these developments in the theoretical domain. Under the tutelage of late Professor H.D. Sankalia, the archaeology faculty of Deccan College in Pune, has taken the lead in experimenting with these new perspectives *vis-à-vis* the country's archaeological record belonging to prehistoric and protohistoric periods. Striking a personal note, since the late 1970s, I have been employing, with some degree of success and satisfaction, perspectives adopted from both the New Archaeology and ideational archaeology in my studies concerning the Palaeolithic and Neolithic cultures of southern Deccan. I have also published a series of papers on this theme in India and outside and a book entitled *The New Archaeology and Aftermath: A View from Outside the Anglo-American World* (1990). Further, I have enjoyed and benefited too from teaching a full course on archaeological theory to successive batches of postgraduate students for well over two decades.

The essays included in the present volume are based on the invited lectures delivered by me after my superannuation in 2008. These were delivered at various places in the country: Sri Venkateswara University, Tirupati; Asiatic Society, Kolkata; Bhandarkar Oriental Research Institute and Deccan College in Pune; Banaras Hindu University, Varanasi; and Institute of Archaeology, Archaeological Survey of India, New Delhi. Chapter I examines the wider background for the growth of New Archaeology and subsequent interpretive trends, and also identifies their principal tenets. The next chapter seeks to relate these developments to Indian archaeology. In chapter III, I use the examples constituted by D.D. Kosambi and others to emphasize that non-professional writings about our past have their own strengths and need to be warmly welcomed and not shunned. Chapter IV focuses attention on the pre-Darwinian notions of progress and development and the impact of Darwinism on empirical sciences including prehistory. In chapter V, I strongly argue for the need to initiate regular research projects for understanding the psychosocial dimensions of the notion of past inherent in the Indian society. The final chapter tackles the tricky topic of the relevance of the past—a theme particularly important in the contemporary world, which is characterized by the contrasting processes of the widening of man's sense of geographical space and shrinking of his mental horizons.

In particular, I address these essays to young faculty and postgraduate students. Arising from the general nature of themes chosen for these lectures, some degree of overlapping of ideas has become unavoidable, for which I seek the indulgence of readers. It is nevertheless my earnest hope that these essays will serve to enhance the realization that understanding the theoretical and sociological underpinnings is as important as exploring and excavating new sites for the growth of archaeological studies in India.

I am grateful to the Librarian and staff of the Deccan College library (Pune) for their unfailing help and assistance. Aryan Books International deserve full compliments for their diligent work.

Pune **K. Paddayya**
Vijayadasami, 13 October 2013

Contents

List of Illustrations

2.2 Subash C. Malik (1932–) delivering the H.D. Sankalia memorial lecture at the Annual Conference of Indian Society for Prehistoric and Quaternary Studies held at Vadodara in November 2012.

2.3 Hasmukh Dhirajlal Sankalia (1908–1989), Founder-Head of the Department of Archaeology at the Deccan College, Pune.

2.4 James Prinsep (1799–1840), Honorary Secretary of The Asiatic Society, Kolkata, who played a pivotal role in the decipherment of the ancient Indian scripts.

2.4a James Prinsep's arrangement of one-line Brahmi inscriptions found on the pillars of Sanchi stupa, most of which end in the two letters—*da* and *nam*. After Prinsep 1837, Plate XXVII. Courtesy: The Asiatic Society, Kolkata.

2.5 Frank Raymond Allchin (1923–2010) of Cambridge University—an outstanding spokesman of South Asian archaeology in the western world.

2.6 Ernest Binfield Havell (1861–1934), Principal of the Calcutta School of Art.

2.7 Ananda Kentish Coomaraswamy (1887–1947), the famed doyen of South Asian art historical studies.

2.8 Nataraja image installed in 2004 at the European Centre for Nuclear Research (CERN), Geneva.

3.1 D.D. Kosambi (1907–1966), the mathematician who "fell into Indology through the roof".

3.2 Mahadev Govind Ranade (1842–1901), an eminent jurist and early nationalist leader.

3.3 Gurudev Rabindranath Tagore (1861–1941), the first Nobel Laureate from Asia.

3.4 Bruce Rich, a noted American attorney and environmentalist.

CHAPTER I

Theory in Archaeology

The New Archaeology and Later Developments

INTRODUCTION

This chapter proposes to examine the major theoretical changes experienced in archaeology during the last half-century. It will be useful to begin with a brief introductory note about the relevance of theory.

Modern academic world is characterized by an unprecedented growth of disciplines and branches thereof. Truly, learning has come to mean 'knowing more and more about less and less.' Unity of knowledge is one perception which endows a sense of meaning and purpose to the whole pursuit of learning. It was a favoured topic among the Ionian philosophers of Greece. Then it received elaborate attention at the hands of Enlightenment thinkers. In the 20th century, unity of knowledge and its promotion were a central concern of the *International Encyclopaedia of Unified Science* proposed by Otto Neurath and his associates (Neurath, Carnap and Morris 1955). The ill-effects of the schism that had nevertheless developed later between scientists and literary intellectuals in England were the theme of

C.P. Snow's famous Rede lecture on "The Two Cultures: A Second Look" delivered at Cambridge in 1959 (Snow 1969).

In more recent times, this theme of the unity of knowledge found a staunch and forceful advocate in the well-known scientist of biological thought, Edward O. Wilson. His book *Consilience: The Unity of Knowledge* (1999) is an earnest plea to all scientists not to mistake individual trees for forest. Empirical sciences (including archaeology) share certain basic features in respect of the nature of subject matter, general methodology and overall goals. All these disciplines deal with one portion or another of the empirical world. The basic methodology they adopt is what is called the scientific method—careful collection of data from the field or in the laboratory; its analysis and description; probing its character; and identifying and explaining its interconnections.

The empirical disciplines rise above the level of common sense and attain the status of science by way of making conceptual clarifications and employing quantitative methods for dealing with enormous quantities of raw data. Sooner or later, theoretical debates are initiated in the various academic disciplines, leading to loss of their innocence. These theoretical debates introduce lively discussions about the conceptual and methodological strengths and weaknesses of the respective disciplines and their larger relevance to the society as such.

In a small chapter of five pages entitled 'The Value of Philosophy', forming part of his book *The Problems of Philosophy* published a hundred years ago, Bertrand Russell put forward cogent arguments about the relevance of philosophizing or theorizing bent of mind (Russell 1976: 89-94). These arguments are worth noting. Russell stated that while physical sciences promote the bodily welfare of mankind, philosophy promotes the good of human mind (Fig. 1.1).

First, philosophy aims at knowledge that gives unity and system to the entire range of sciences through a critical examination of the grounds of our convictions, prejudices and beliefs. Secondly, while it does not envisage final answers, philosophy poses higher order spiritual questions like whether the universe has any unity of plan and purpose. Thirdly, philosophy underscores the need to replace the principle of certainty with uncertainty in one's outlook. In Russell's own words:

Fig. 1.1 Bertrand Arthur William Russell (1872–1970), the British philosopher of international repute.

> Man is generally imprisoned in the prejudices derived from common sense, from the habitual beliefs of his age or nation, and from convictions which have grown up in his mind without much reason. To such a man the world becomes definite, finite, obvious; common objects rouse no questions, and unfamiliar possibilities are contemptuously rejected. As soon as we begin to philosophize, on the contrary, we find... that even the most everyday things lead to problems to which only very incomplete answers can be given. Philosophy, though unable to tell us with certainty what is the true answer to the doubts which it raises, is able to suggest many possibilities which enlarge our thoughts and free them from the tyranny of custom... (1976: 91).

Finally, philosophic contemplation enables man to rise above the level of instinctive life habits and enables union of the human mind with the universe itself.

Russell's propositions about the importance of philosophy give us a perspective to initiate a discussion about the role of theory in archaeology. Theory fulfils several important watch-dog functions. The principal ones among these are as follows:

a) Continuous debate about the nature, scope and goals of archaeology.
b) Clarifications about the conceptual apparatus of the discipline. Gordon Childe (1956: 69-95) termed this component as categories, which serve as constructional tools for framing knowledge about the past.
c) Continuous discussions about the methodological aspects of archaeological research, covering what Wheeler (1949: 4) called strategies and tactics.
d) Examination of the historiographical aspects of archaeological investigations.
e) Analysis of sociological and psychological factors affecting archaeological studies.
f) Discussions about the larger social relevance of heritage studies.

As told by Glyn Daniel (1967, 1975) and Bruce Trigger (1989), the discipline has a long story but its history is short. Its beginnings go back to the various antiquarian studies undertaken in Europe from the 16th to 18th centuries. As an organized quest for knowledge about the past, it emerged only during the 19th century. By announcing his Three-Age System, C.J. Thomsen of the Royal Danish Museum in Copenhagen laid the true foundations of modern archaeology. Heinrich Schliemann and

Flinders Petrie added Bronze Age Civilizations to the list of ancient cultures. Also, archaeology was introduced in the university curriculum by the end of the 19th century. In the first half of the following century, there came up many more discoveries concerning hunting-gathering and agropastoral cultures as well as Bronze Age Civilizations. No less important, thanks to the efforts of Gordon Childe (1956), Grahame Clark (1960), Gordon Willey and P. Phillips (1958), and others, the conceptual basis of the discipline was also built up.

The topic of conceptual structure of the discipline came up for elaborate discussion and debate from the 1960s. First came up the New Archaeology with its emphasis on systemic and adaptational conceptions of culture and the need to view the past in terms of cultural processes and patterns. This became the rage among workers for two decades or so and continues in its various versions to be a dominant paradigm in contemporary archaeology. But already from the 1980s some fresh trends began to set in; these coalesced into what may be called interpretive archaeology. As in the case of the New Archaeology, interpretive archaeology too experienced the growth of several sub-trends. These developments also brought to the fore sociological dimensions or public domain of the discipline.

In a famous article entitled "Archaeology: The Loss of Innocence", the late David Clarke (1973) identified four qualitative stages in the development of archaeology. These are the stages of consciousness, self-consciousness, critical self-consciousness and self-critical self-consciousness. Consciousness is the stage when the discipline was named. The stage of self-consciousness experienced further developments in the form of specification of concepts and methods and also appearance of textbooks and journals. The stage of critical self-consciousness sought to elevate the status of archaeology beyond the level of an 'undisciplined empirical discipline' by introducing intense theoretical debates about the nature of knowledge and reasoning processes. The stage of self-critical self-consciousness was one of a more mature and intense analysis of the goals, methods and sociological dimensions of the study of the past. Although Clarke himself did not make any suggestions to this effect, I am tempted to say that these four stages correlate, respectively, with the stages of antiquarianism, natural history or culture history, the New Archaeology, and rise of post-processual or interpretive archaeology. Let us now take up the latter two stages for a more detailed study.

THE NEW ARCHAEOLOGY

I shall touch upon the following major aspects of the New Archaeology: a) the overall academic ferment that prevailed in social sciences in the mid-20th century; b) how it facilitated or even anticipated the growth of a nonconformist movement in archaeology; c) reconceptualization of theoretical and methodological domains of the whole discipline; d) growth of sub-schools within the New Archaeology; and e) some examples of field research from both New and Old Worlds involving the application of the New Archaeology's formulations in theory and method.

BACKGROUND

Far from constituting an aberration, the rise of the New Archaeology fits in very well with our knowledge of the history of major developments in both natural and social sciences, all continuously striving to achieve a more systematic and comprehensive understanding of the whats, wheres, whens, hows and whys of specific portions of the empirical world forming their subject matter. One general feature that strikes us is that all these disciplines were initially preoccupied with singular-atomistic studies, which were subsequently replaced by perspectives treating phenomena as *Ganzheiten* or interconnected wholes.

Secondly, in their formative stages, these sciences primarily concerned themselves with the identification of broad, long-term trends about their respective domains of the empirical world. Soon a need was felt to put these sweeping ideas on a sounder basis by taking up systematic studies of spatially and temporally limited portions of reality. In physical sciences, the experimental method played an important role in these fresh studies since the beginning of the 18th century. Commenting on its role, Heisenberg (1952:79) wrote: "This method could be applied to individual problems posed by nature and hence it was no longer a question of understanding a single interconnected whole but of a detailed analysis of many small specific connections." Highlighting a similar situation that prevailed in the social sciences, the 19th-century French sociologist-philosopher Tarde averred: "... a new science begins by assuming the existence of large-scale 'apparent' regularities, but can genuinely advance only with the discovery of the real, small-scale repetitions" (as quoted by Martindale 1961: 446).

It was against this wider background that many of the social sciences took new incarnations towards the end of the 19th century and in the first half of the next century. New Geography, New History, New Sociology, New Anthropology, New Political Science, etc. appeared on the academic horizon.

In its antiquarian stages, archaeology too was concerned with particular sites and monuments and then started recognizing broad, long-term trends in the preliterate past of humankind.

C.J. Thomsen's Three-Age System—Stone, Bronze, and Iron Ages—was the first step in this direction (Thomsen 1848). These Ages were much elaborated and improved upon in the second half of the 19th century by John Lubbock and other workers in Europe. Benefiting from the recognition of these stages and also from the archaeological discoveries made in the first half of the 20th century, several evolutionary or developmental models of the preliterate stage were put forward. Publications such as Gordon Childe's *Man Makes Himself* (1936) and *What Happened in History* (1942), and Leslie White's *The Evolution of Culture: The Development of Civilization to the Fall of Rome* (1959) not only strengthened the discipline's academic identity and brought the story of humankind to the threshold of educated layperson but also gave a fillip to regional archaeological investigations in both Old and New Worlds. Thus, culture history, involving the preparation of regional timetables of culture, emerged as a dominant trend by the mid-20th century.

Cultures were defined as recurrent series of similar-looking artefactual assemblages having spatio-temporal boundaries. The introduction of various scientific techniques and methods after World War II added an extra dimension to the study of archaeological record (Brothwell and Higgs 1963). Wherever large-scale excavations were undertaken, it was even possible to say something about the past lifeways. In short, many queries about the whats, whens and wheres of the archaeological record were raised and successfully answered. Soon some books devoted to theory and method also appeared, such as Grahame Clark's *Archaeology and Society* (1939), Gordon Childe's *Piecing together the Past* (1956), Willey and Phillips's *Method and Theory in American Archaeology* (1958), and Stuart Piggott's *Approach to Archaeology* (1959).

These positive developments, while they constituted what David Clarke (1973) called the stage of self-consciousness, were not without their sceptics. Clarke (1968: xiii) himself called the whole endeavour "an undisciplined empirical discipline". The issue for the discipline was epistemological in nature and necessitated a re-examination of its foundations and a logical analysis of its concepts. In other words, questions were raised about the quality of knowledge itself about the past. Could one elevate this knowledge from the level of data-packed, inductive generalizations or assortments of facts to that of seeking interconnections among these facts? Observations like the one made by the French film-maker Louis Renoir that "I care not for things themselves but their interconnections" began to find echo in archaeological circles too. Gordon Childe (1935) and John Bennett (1943) called attention to the task of reading meanings of the archaeological record in functional terms (Fig. 1.2). In his Rickett memorial lecture of 1953, Grahame Clark (Fig. 1.3) diagrammatically represented human culture as made up of various structural components, all linked one with another and with the environment (Clark 1960: 175). Walter Taylor's (1948) book *A Study of Archaeology* not only advocated contextual and functional approaches to the analysis of archaeological data but in fact anticipated the more recent interpretive trends by locating the source of behaviour in human minds and the various feelings and

Fig. 1.2 Vere Gordon Childe (1892–1957), Founder-Director of the Institute of Archaeology, London.

Fig. 1.3 Sir John Grahame Douglas Clark (1907–1995), Disney Professor of Archaeology in Cambridge University, explaining faunal finds at Star Carr excavation.

sentiments generated there (Fig. 1.4). Julian Steward's (1955) cultural ecology stressed the need for monitoring interconnections between cultural and environmental components. Willey and Phillips (1958) called for an anthropological orientation to the whole discipline (Fig. 1.5).

But all these views and ideas were in the form of isolated pleas for improvement and, therefore, failed to make any significant impact on the archaeological community. It was left to the proponents of the New Archaeology to coalesce these "germs of thought" and add to these the hardware as formed by statistical techniques for pattern-recognition and the software as provided by principles of the scientific method. Once this fusion took place, a virtual manifesto was born, as contained in the

Fig. 1.4 Walter Willard Taylor (1913–1997), author of *A Study of Archaeology* (1948).

Fig. 1.5 Gordon Randolph Willey (1913–2002) of Harvard University and Viru Valley settlement pattern study fame.

initial writings of Lewis Binford (1962, 1964, 1965, 1968a) and David Clarke (1968, 1973). One is reminded here of the analogy provided by the famous pamphlet of 1929 issued by the Vienna Circle, which wanted to free empirical sciences from the "metaphysical and theological debris of millennia" and inject into these a scientific world-conception (wissenschaftliche Auffassung) (Hahn 1929). Archaeology simply represents the latest example among empirical sciences, which experienced this shift from a mere concern with bundles of facts to the construction of positivist and verifiable knowledge about the real world. It is unimaginable that, without the background provided by this fundamental change, the ideational trends that later arrived in archaeology would have found a rationale for their genesis.

BIRTH OF THE NEW ARCHAEOLOGY

The actual genesis of the New Archaeology took place in the 1960s. Not many feathers will be ruffled when it is said that the *dramatis personae* comprise just two figures—David Clarke from England and Lewis Binford from the U.S. Let us first consider the views of Clarke (Fig. 1.6). He introduced statistical methods to understand variability in the archaeological record, be they simple artefacts or megalithic tombs. By means of matrix analysis Clarke recognized two main geographical or functional series within the British Beaker pottery dated to the 3rd millennium BC (Clarke 1962). In 1968, he published his book *Analytical Archaeology*, which sought to revamp the whole conceptual framework of the discipline. Of particular importance is his conception of cultures as systems consisting of components interacting among themselves and with the environmental subsystems.

Fig. 1.6 David L. Clarke (1938-1976) of Cambridge University, British proponent of the New Archaeology.

His paper "Archaeology: The loss of innocence" was a terse (hence termed gobbledygook by readers in Britain) but welcome exposition of the major tenets of the new stream of thought (Clarke 1973). As mentioned earlier, he identified four stages in the development archaeology, viz., stages of consciousness, self-consciousness, critical self-consciousness, and self-critical self-consciousness. He also advocated the study and interpretation of archaeological record with reference to four paradigms (morphological, geographical, anthropological, and ecological). Clarke visualized that the application of these paradigms would lead to improvements in theory formation at four levels: concepts, information, reasoning, and general theory. These views reflect Clarke's larger conception of the archaeological record in cultural and anthropological terms. Finally, he defined the New Archaeology as "an interpenetrating set of new methods, new observations, new paradigms, new philosophies, and new ideologies within a new environment" (Clarke 1973: 12). His death in 1976 at the young age of 38 robbed archaeology of one of its most fertile minds.

Binford's (Fig. 1.7) contribution to the emergence of the New Archaeology was as much an expression of the mind inspired by ideas about the relevance of scientific reasoning and statistical techniques for pattern-recognition as it was the product of clashes of ideas with senior colleagues like James Griffin and Robert Braidwood at the universities of Michigan and Chicago about the nature of archaeological record and its potentialities to inform us about the past. The introductory portions of the

Fig. 1.7 Lewis Roberts Binford (1931–2011), North American proponent of the New Archaeology.

three volumes containing his collected essays (Binford 1972a, 1983a, 1989) and also the inside-view provided by one of his group members (Flannery 2006) provide many gripping details of the birth pangs as well as of later developments concerning the New Archaeology's efforts to direct attention to the larger anthropological goals of the discipline (Willey and Sabloff 1980: 181-210; O'Brien, Lyman and Schiffer 2005: 36-66). Binford (1972a: 1-14) told us how his stint of military service in East Asia created in him an interest in observing simple societies, which in turn motivated him to enroll for a graduate programme in anthropology, and how he developed an 'archaeology commitment' in order to provide a temporal perspective for explaining diversity in human societies across the globe. He also told us about the clashes he had with senior archaeologists about the very definition of concepts like culture, the whys and hows of the emergence of food-producing way of life, and explanation of variability in archaeological record.

Structure of the New Archaeology

With this background we shall now identify the main propositions of the New Archaeology. It should be noted at this stage that the phrase New Archaeology was a pejorative expression used by critics for lumping together the unconventional papers that were being presented by Binford and his group at meetings of the Society for American Archaeology in the early 1960s. Binford himself was content with characterizing the views of his group as "New Perspectives" that call for "some fundamental changes in the way archaeologists viewed the archaeological record and particularly in the conventions then current for assigning meaning to archaeological facts" (Binford 1986: 459). But the label got entrenched in the literature.

Conceptual Changes

The New Archaeology argued for a basic epistemological change (see Wylie 2002: 57-77). In traditional archaeology, facts *per se*—be these about dates, sizes of sites or the actual finds—constituted knowledge and were regarded as self-explanatory. These only required to be organized into assortments or groups. Generalizations in the form of summaries of facts constituted knowledge about the past, e.g. culture X has red and grey ceramic fabrics in equal proportions, represented by 13 and 16 vessel shapes respectively. The New Archaeology raised questions about the usefulness of this form of knowledge in promoting the cause of anthropological orientation to archaeological record. As Bertrand Russell would have argued, can we meaningfully understand the world around us by merely enumerating its 'furniture'? The anthropological dimension, involving the study of development of human cultural forms along space and time trajectories, required the archaeologists to thread their facts together. Adopting the age-old saying 'Divided we fall, united we stand', the new epistemological turn laid emphasis on linkages among facts.

This epistemological reorientation entailed two drastic changes in the culture concept. First, in the place of the earlier "shreds and patches" and trait-list versions, cultures now began to be treated as totalities or systems comprising not merely component elements but their interrelationships as well. Secondly, the normative definition of culture as a repository of ideas and norms held in the minds of people was now substituted by a functional definition treating it as an extrasomatic means of adaptation. Butzer (1982) independently discussed at length the operational strategies required for putting the concept of adaptation to use.

This redefinition of culture highlighted the study of culture process, which has become synonymous with the New Archaeology.

In order to emphasize the importance of anthropological orientation to the discipline advocated by him, in the initial stages Binford did talk of archaeology's contribution to the understanding of diachronic or long-term trends in the evolution of culture and even hinted at the possibility of tracking down 'laws of cultural dynamics'. But it was soon realized that this task must be preceded by a more fundamental task—that of holistic understanding of spatially and temporarily limited segments of the archaeological record. This required a shift of emphasis from the study of culture of humankind to the investigation of cultures of peoples. It is the study of this synchronic aspect of culture which constitutes culture process; it finds expression at numerous places in the writings of both Clarke and Binford. Clarke derived inspiration from cybernetics developed by Norbert Wiener. On his part Binford was influenced by General Systems Theory advocated by Ludwig Von Bertalanffy and other workers (see essays in Emery 1969; a similar framework called tektology was developed earlier by the Russian scientist Alexander Bogdanov, see Blauberg, Sadovsky and Yudin 1977) and the ecosystem approaches of Eugene Odum (1963, 1971) and other biologists, which had already emerged as prominent research orientations in the empirical sciences (for a lengthy and non-technical discussion, see Capra 1977: Chapters 1 to 4).

A few additional remarks are warranted on this issue of culture process. David Clarke (1968: Chapters 2 and 3) viewed archaeological cultures as vast information systems, made up of several interlinked subsystems. He viewed the aim of archaeology as the identification of patterns or regularities in the functioning of cultural systems, which in turn would lead to a higher body of knowledge in the form of models and hypotheses. Binford espoused the culture process concept in more elaborate terms.

Writing in 1968, Binford stated: "Process, as I understand it, refers to the dynamic relationships (causes and effects) operative among the components of a system or between systemic components and the environment" (Binford 1972a: 117). Some years later, he warned: "A cultural system is not a summation of all the events, behaviours or other transactional phenomena going on at a given time, but rather the conditioning organizational framework within which all these events transpire" (Binford 1981a: 201). Later, Binford underlined the priority of the study of process at synchronic level in the following words:

> ... before archaeologists could cite formal variability in the archaeological record as indicative of large-scale process, evolution, system changes, ethnicity, or even such historical events as migrations, we had to be able to recognize the archaeological record at differing organizational scales (Binford 1989: 18).

Thus, in their advocacy of the cause of culture process, neither Clarke nor Binford showed any interest in producing yet another grand model of cultural evolution. Rather, their interest was in 'freezing' cultural systems in space and time in order to understand their functioning. This synchronic process-orientation of the New Archaeology was influenced by the prevailing functionalist trends in anthropology via the writings of Leslie White and others. As stated earlier, it constitutes a major instance of the operation of two important trends noticed in the history of factual sciences. These are: a) coming into vogue of theories treating phenomena as *Ganzheiten* in replacement of singular-atomistic studies; and

b) shift of emphasis from the formulation of linear or long-term trends to the detection of constant, short-term relationships and uniformities. It is woth noting here that processual orientation to the study of social phenomena was already a prominent feature of the American social sciences like sociology, political science and economics in the early part of the 20th century (Kress 1970).

Methodological Innovations

In order to give effect to these radical conceptual changes, the New Archaeology proposed innovations in the methodological approaches or strategies to be adopted for studying the archaeological record at various levels. Realizing that cultural systems of whatever age always operate at a regional level but never exclusively at the level of individual sites—however big these might be, a Cahokia or a Troy or a Harappa—Binford called for the employment of a regional research strategy in the field investigations. In his own words:

> It is argued that the methodology most appropriate to the study of culture process is a regional approach in which we attempt to gain reliable and representative information covering the internal structure and ecological systems (Binford 1964: 160).

The archaeological record was now visualized as consisting of populations of cultural items, cultural features, sites, and ecofacts or non-artefactual data of cultural significance. Since it is not always possible to exhaustively study all portions or aspects of regional or site data, the New Archaeology for the first time introduced probability sampling methods and multi-stage fieldwork into the discipline for identifying and studying representative units of data universe.

As a complement to these innovations in field strategies, the New Archaeology also called for a more rigorous analysis of the archaeological record itself. Reference has already been made to Clarke's use of matrix analysis for restudying the British Beaker pottery. Under Albert Spaulding's tutelage, Binford acquired familiarity with multivariate statistical techniques, which proved to be extremely helpful to him in identifying patterns in the archaeological record and also in inferring similarities and differences among cultural systems.

These innovations in field methodology and data analysis were pooled together by Binford to develop a research paradigm called the settlement system approach (Binford and Binford 1969). While settlement pattern studies stop at the level of descriptive account of distribution of sites on a given patch of landscape (Willey 1953; Chang 1968), the settlement system approach is explanatory in nature and seeks to lay bare the linkages between site contexts, resource use schedule, demographic arrangement and ecological setting. While neighbouring human groups may share similar genetic, linguistic and historical traditions, they nevertheless tend to develop their own settlement systems due to differences in both natural and social environments. Initially, the settlement system approach was developed by Binford to explain variability in the French Mousterian assemblages. This work and his prolonged ethnoarchaeological study of the Nunamiut Eskimos of Alaska enabled him to formulate the forager versus collector model of hunter-gatherer settlement systems (Binford 1980). His more recent book *Constructing Frames of Reference: An Analytical Method for Archaeological Theory Building* (2001) extended this model to cover about 340 hunter-gatherer societies spread across the world. With some additions and variations, it is also applicable to the study of food-producing and other developed cultural systems.

Role of Scientific Reasoning

There are two important and overarching aspects of the New Archaeology—both falling within the domain of scientific reasoning (Paddayya 1983, 1990: 8-19). One of these concerns the nature and role of laws or generalizations in archaeological research. This topic generated much debate in the discipline and to some extent even scandalized the New Archaeology by caricaturing its proponents as 'a law and order group.' During my visit to one of the universities in Midwest America in 1999, I noticed on the chamber door of a senior faculty member this short inscription: "All generalizations are false." This hostile attitude to the topic was occasioned by certain misconceptions: a) traditional archaeology's relativistic and trait-list conceptions of human cultures, providing no scope for generalizations; b) the supposedly inviolable nature of law-like propositions in natural sciences; and c) the unwarranted view that laws in archaeology must refer to long-term trends in human culture.

Such misconceptions are totally uncalled for on various counts. First, laws do not exist in nature but are conventions made by us to designate recurring patterns or associations (causal and otherwise) among phenomena. Secondly, there is no finality attached to them, since the empirical world is infinite and new data could at any time necessitate revision or even discard of existing generalizations. So the inscription on the door of the American professor's chamber should more appropriately read: "All generalizations are false and are liable to be replaced by newer ones." Thirdly, generalizations are not ends in themselves but form "an indispensable instrument of historical research" (Hempel 1965: 231). Mandelbaum (1977) aptly called them the 'mortar' of historical accounts. Fourthly, the oft-repeated dichotomy that socio-cultural sciences are idiographic (seekers of individual facts) and that natural sciences are nomothetic or law-making, is totally false. The fact is that research in all empirical sciences presupposes an unending cycle between acquisition of facts and threading them together with the help of generalizations. Hence, both groups of sciences are idiographic as well as nomothetic. There is absolutely no way that archaeology can be excluded from this matrix and accorded a special status.

As pointed out by Hempel (1965: 242-43), past-related sciences like history and archaeology do make use of pre-scientific generalizations of everyday experience as well as generalizations adopted from both social and natural sciences. Archaeology has made its own generalizations, e.g. Three-Age System, law of evolutionary potential, law of cultural dominance, etc. (Stickel and Chartkoff 1973).

Middle Range Theory, as developed by Lewis Binford, seeks to identify more of such general propositions (Arnold III 2003). It rises above the earlier, arbitrary ways of giving meanings to the archaeological record and aims to develop a fresh cognitive frame of reference. This cognitive framework consists of ideas and concepts in terms of which one could diagnose the archaeological record in order to identify the processes that led to its formation (Binford 1977, 1981). Binford visualized that Middle Range Theory (encompassing ethnoarchaeological research, use-wear analyses, and bone taphonomy) could produce patterns at three levels: a) first-order field or laboratory observations about various segments of the archaeological record; b) second-order observations recognizing patterns between two or more variables; and c) pattern-recognition leading to theory formation which establishes causal links in cultural systems and explain their functioning. Middle Range Theory paves the way for General Theory which has the task of "understanding the processes responsible for change and diversification in the organizational properties of living systems" (Binford 1977: 7).

Binford's book *Constructing Frames of Reference: An Analytical Method for Archaeological Theory Building* (2001) contains a large number of lower, middle and higher order generalizations arrived at after a comparative study of all major hunter-gatherer societies of the world. Referring to their possible use to archaeologists, Binford (2001: 3) writes:

> ...From the equations developed in the book an archaeologist can anticipate many of the properties of hunter-gatherer groups that might be expected to occur at a given location, at an archaeological site or at a series of sites... the explanatory theory is available for archaeologists to use deductively by reasoning to or simulating changing conditions and thereby providing patterns of change that can be expected to occur in the archaeological record at specific locations...

Another major contribution made by the New Archaeology to the discipline relates to the introduction of the method of hypothesis testing. Traditional archaeology relied mainly on the use of intuitive observations and *ex cathedra* statements. Attention was now called for the need to test the reliability of archaeological reconstructions. For this purpose, the method of hypothesis forming part of philosophy of science was adopted. In Binford's own words:

> The accuracy of our knowledge of past can be measured; it is this assertion which most sharply differentiates the new perspectives from more traditional approaches. The yardstick of measurement is the degree to which propositions about the past can be confirmed or refuted through hypothesis-testing (Binford 1972a: 90).

Although one could locate some instances of hypothesis formulation in traditional archaeology, e.g. Thomsen calling his Three-Age System a conjecture to be confirmed or rejected in the light of future work, and the Iraq Jarmo project of Robert Braidwood (1974) for ascertaining Neolithic origins, New Archaeology called for a formal introduction of the hypothetico-deductive method in order to deal with the problem of whys and hows of culture process. It involves putting forward a hypothetical answer to a problematic situation concerning the archaeological record and deducing from it consequences which could be tested with reference to the empirical world. In natural sciences, the application of this method led to far-reaching qualitative changes in knowledge formation.

In fact, the method of hypothesis is adopted even in day-to-day life for coming to grips with practical issues: The 19th century British administrator of the Deccan Meadows Taylor provides a fine example. In his autobiography *The Story of My Life*, Taylor says that he had "formed a little plan of my own which I longed to test" for putting an end to the turbulent political relationships that prevailed between the Bedar chiefs of Shorapur principality, the princely State of the Nizam of Hyderabad of which it was a part, and the Biritsh (Taylor 1989: 123). Once he was able to convince the recalcitrant Bedar chiefs that his mission as the Political Agent had nothing to do with the imposition of the British power but was aimed at putting in place the overall administration of the principality. Taylor was soon accepted by the chiefs as their friend and then truly dedicated himself for well over a decade to improving the welfare of the people. His work in this part of the Deccan forms a glorious chapter in the history of colonial administration.

As with the topic of laws, the method of hypothesis too invited much doubt and disbelief in archaeology in the initial stages. The reason being traditional archaeology had by and large been content with answering questions of what, when and where by making inductive statements taking the form of summaries of facts. The scope for raising why and how queries was limited. Moreover it was mistakenly believed that hypotheses should always involve 'if, then' causal links. The truth is that research in empirical sciences has much scope for and needs non-causal hypotheses too. The Greek philosopher Novalis put this issue very well: "Hypotheses are like nets; only he who casts, will catch" (Popper 1980:11). In our own times the French scientist Poincaré tendered this useful advice:

> Instead of summary condemnation we should examine with the utmost care the role of hypothesis; we shall then recognize not only that it is necessary, but that in most cases it is legitimate. We shall also see that there are several kinds of hypotheses; that some are verifiable, and when once confirmed by experiment, become truths of great fertility; that others may be useful to us in fixing our ideas, and finally, that others are hypotheses only in appearance, and reduce to definitions or to conventions in disguise (as quoted in Copi and Gould 1972: 284).

Estimates of the place of the New Archaeology vary. James Griffin (1985) observed total silence about it while reviewing his career achievements in archaeology. Walter Taylor (1972) called these ideas 'old wine in new skins'. In contrast to this opinion, another senior archaeologist Paul Martin (1972) called the New Archaeology a revolution. But this has been denied by Meltzer (1979); he believes that it represents a continuum with traditional perspectives (see also Wylie 2002: 25-41).

Revolution or not, the New Archaeology represents a set of eclectic conceptual and methodological tenets aimed at a reorientation of our basic perceptions of the archaeological record. The following are the principal new perceptions:

a) Systemic conception of cultures in the place of the traditional type-fossil and trait-list views;
b) Emphasis on knowing how cultures function with reference to their own components as well as surrounding environmental and social milieu;
c) Adoption of a regional perspective in field studies;
d) Use of various pattern-recognition techniques;
e) Emphasis on the use of generalizations secured via Middle Range Theory; and
f) Application of the method of hypothesis.

All these were geared to raise knowledge of the past from the level of accumulation of individual facts to the status of science that seeks to identify their interconnections and explain their whys and hows (Wylie 1981; Watson 1991; Gamble 1999; Meltzer 2011). The New Archaeology thus achieved the effect of 'lowering of foundations' of the discipline and brought in a new paradigm in the sense of "a universally recognized scientific achievement that for a time provides model problems and solutions to a community of practitioners" (Kuhn 1962: x).

Growth of 'Newer' Archaeologies

Notwithstanding all these innovations, the New Archaeology failed to remain a unified stream of thought. Influenced or inspired by it in one way or another, several 'newer' archaeologies appeared on the American scene from the 1970s onwards. These include an 'explicitly scientific' archaeology (Watson *et al.* 1971), behavioural archaeology of Michael Schiffer, cultural materialism (Segraves 1974), Marxist archaeologies (Spriggs 1984), critical archaeology (Leone, Potter and Shackel 1987), *Annales* perspectives (Knapp 1992), cognitive processual archaeology (Renfrew 1994), and evolutionary archaeologies (Maschner 1996; O'Brien and Lyman 2000). While conceding the importance of processual orientation provided to the discipline by the New Archaeology and also its efforts to strengthen the discipline's conceptual foundations, these 'newer' perspectives sought to attend to some of the gaps left untouched by the main programme (see Wylie 2002: 78-96).

Among these, behavioural archaeology, as developed by Michael Schiffer, is a more prominent and enduring one. Schiffer successfully argued that inferring human behaviour from archaeological record entails us to first recognize the processes involved in the transformation of objects from one state to another within the original systemic or living context and then their transfer to the archaeological context (Schiffer 1976). He also pointed out that archaeologists paid no attention to the possible cultural as well as natural processes that acted upon the archaeological record since its disconnection with its creators. Thus, Schiffer highlighted for the first time the need to understand the processes that create as well as transform the archaeological record before we use it for reconstructing past human behaviour (Schiffer 1995). It is not surprising therefore that the topic of formation processes (*c*-transforms and *n*-transforms) has become an integral component of contemporary archaeology's suite of research strategies (Schiffer 1987).

Impact

Let us briefly consider the impact made by the New Archaeology on the discipline. Its theoretical and methodological propositions made sense particularly to those who were actively involved in the study of archaeological record in the field or laboratory and who desired to pull out interconnections of various kinds from the 'teeth of stubborn and irresistible' facts. Citation of a few studies carried out at site or regional levels will be useful. Let us start with the contributions of the two architects themselves.

Two of David Clarke's reinterpretations of the European archaeological record are fascinating examples of model building. First, his restudy of the archaeological record of the British Iron Age site of Glastonbury, which was excavated three quarters of a century ago. His efforts to infer "mutual relationships and the strengths and covariation of those relationships in a variety of alternative classificatory dimensions" led him to slot this small Iron Age site at a lower level of the four-tier settlement (and impliedly social) hierarchy that existed in the marshlands of Somerset (Clarke 1972). The second study concerns the nature of economic organization of the North European Mesolithic phase. Clarke carefully examined the functional aspect of microlithic assemblages and also the implications of the spurt in vegetative growth that followed upon the retreat of ice-sheets from the North European plains. This led him to doubt the emphasis on hunting that had been placed by earlier archaeologists. Instead, he proposed the view that the Mesolithic subsistence economy "may have approached limited, fire-controlled asexual horticulture and arboriculture, based on vegetatively reproducing *root* staples, forest *perennials*, controlled nut and fruit trees, backed up by shell-fish, dog and pig husbandry…" (Clarke 1978: 36).

Binford's first major use of the new armature for approaching the archaeological record concerned the four or five variants that had been recognized by Francois Bordes within the French Mousterian. Raising serious objections to Bordes' interpretations equating the variants with different ethnic groups, he and his wife Sally Binford put forward the famous functional argument which sought to trace assemblage variability to functional variability, which in turn is governed by seasonal variability in the availability of resources (Binford and Binford 1966). This argument was extended to account for variability in the Late Acheulian assemblages from Olorgesailie, Kalambo Falls and other sites in Africa (Binford 1972b). Later, Binford used this strategy and re-examined the faunal collections obtained much earlier from Olduvai Gorge localities in East Africa from the point of view of bone taphonomy and arrived at the startling conclusion that the early hominins, far from being great hunters, were only scavengers of the left-overs of meat from carnivore kill sites (Binford 1981b; 1983b). Likewise, the mighty 'elephant-hunters' of Torralba were reduced to the status of mere expedient exploiters of animal food resources naturally available in the ecosystem (Binford 1987). These studies provided much stimulus to contemporary research on bone taphonomy and hominin dietary patterns.

Likewise, in his paper 'Post-Pleistocene Adaptations' Binford (1968b) reviewed evidence pertaining to origins of food-producing ways of life. Going beyond 'nuclear zone' and 'culture was ripe' theories, he put forward the view that in the Near East, evidence of primary level plant and animal domestication would be found not in the areas occupied by sedentary forager-fisher groups but in the adjacent zones. He further pointed that evidence for independent experiments in food production could be expected from various areas in both New and Old Worlds—a proposition upheld by a series of field projects undertaken subsequently.

The Mousterian debate with Bordes made Binford realize the need to supplement archaeological data with analogies drawn from the study of actual functioning of living hunter-gatherer societies. His four-year-long (1969 to 1973) field studies among the Nunamiut Eskimos of Alaska and the resulting publication set a model for later work in hunter-gatherer ethnoarchaeology (Binford 1978). It has already been mentioned that the settlement system approach to archaeological record developed by him is a lasting contribution to the discipline and, with suitable modifications and additions, is helpful for studying the structure and functioning of even agropastoral and other later cultures.

We will now examine the use of new ideas by other archaeologists. The volume *New Perspectives in Archaeology*, edited by Sally and Lewis Binford (1968), contains a set of ten papers presented at a symposium organized in Denver in 1965 as part of the annual conference of American Anthropological Association. These papers represent the first-generation applications of the New Archaeology in the Americas. Irven DeVore, one of the seven leading non-archaeological anthropologists of the time who had been invited to comment on these papers, summed up the overall positive response in these words:

> ...I warmly applaud the shift in emphasis in archaeological thinking in recent years as evidenced, for example, by the papers in this symposium. In the past we were presented with lithic industries which, to judge by their descriptions, were copulating, hybridizing, evolving, adapting, and producing offspring ... (DeVore 1968:346).

The papers by James Deetz, William Longacre, James Hill and Robert Whallon used ceramic data from individual American archaeological sites to make inferences about social organization (demographic aspects, and residence and descent rules). The papers by Howard Winters, Kent Flannery and Michael Coe, and Stuart Struever, also dealing with North American sites, were broader in scope and region-oriented. More importantly, these papers adopted ecosystem and functionalist orientations for studying the archaeological record of the Formative and Classic stages. This volume also included three papers which took the new ideas to the Old World—Sally Binford's paper on variability in the Near Eastern Mousterian, James Sackett's paper on the French Upper Palaeolithic, and Frank Hole's study of the early food-producing culture of Iran.

Coincidentally, another set of eight interesting essays appeared in 1968 as part of an edited volume entitled *Anthropological Archaeology in the Americas* (Meggers 1968). These essays, arising from lectures delivered during the two previous years under the auspices of the Anthropological Society of Washington, were very much in alignment with the new ideas that were already in the air. In fact, three of the writers also published papers in *New Perspectives* as mentioned above. These contributions once again laid emphasis on systemic and superorganic conceptions of culture and the role of the natural environment. Stuart Struever argued for a methodological reorientation in American archaeology in order to come to grips with the new goals. James Deetz's essay dealt with issues relating to the contact period. The remaining six papers (by J. Campbell, E. Wilmsen, J. Schoenwetter and A. Dithert Jr., K.V. Flannery, W. Sanders and D. Thompson) reflected the use of new ideas and methods in the investigation of American archaeological sites belonging to palaeo-Indian and later cultural stages.

Subsequently, some of the above-mentioned authors elaborated on these beginnings and completed major research projects, e.g. Flannery's (1976, 1986) work on the early food-producing cultures of the southern highlands of Mexico and Winters' (1969) work on the Riverton culture of Wabash Valley in Illinois. Other major projects, which also fall within the framework of the New Archaeology, include the work of MacNeish and others on the emergence of food-producing way of life in the Tehuacan Valley (MacNeish *et al.* 1972) and Adams' work in Mesopotamia (1965, 1966; Adams and Nissen 1972).

The volume *Processual Archaeology*, edited by Johnson (2004), contains a set of another ten essays representing third-generation studies employing the approaches recommended by the New Archaeology. These concern site- or regional-level studies of sites belonging to hunter-gatherer and later stages and clearly show that the themes broached by the New Archaeology are still vibrant in contemporary archaeology both in America and the Old World. Surely, between 1968 and the volume edited by Johnson, there have been a good number of field studies of hunter-gatherer, food-producing and state- level societies in different parts of the world which benefited from the New Archaeology's propositions (O'Brien, Lyman and Schiffer 2005: Chapters 3 and 4). But it may as well be the case that, just as one does not invariably notice Darwin's name in the discussions concerning theory of evolution, the inspiration provided by the New Archaeology does not find explicit mention in all cases.

POST-PROCESSUAL OR INTERPRETIVE ARCHAEOLOGY

Scientific research is a dynamic and trial-and-error process. It always builds further upon existing blocks of knowledge, conceptual or factual. We have noted earlier how already in the

1970s several sub-trends began to crop up in the North American New Archaeology. It is worth noting here that these sub-trends, while they deviated from the main perspective in respect of minor details, shared with it almost all traits of positivistic knowledge—importance of objectivity, systematic character, need for precision and exactness, role of hypothesis, etc. All these sub-trends advocated a hard approach to the archaeological record inasmuch as these treated human cultures as adaptational mechanisms developed by people for coping up with their respective environmental settings.

But the succeeding decade witnessed the rise of what may be called interpretive archaeology claiming itself to be an alternative to processual archaeology. Now a 'soft' approach began to be put forward to the archaeological record. It was no longer treated as a mere physical entity but began to be viewed as a text whose meanings need to be read by archaeologists (Patrik 1985). That is, some archaeologists began to argue that archaeology cannot stop at the level of reconstructing past human behaviour from archaeological record but should be able to trace it back to the human mind and various feelings, sentiments and emotions that emanate from it. This new stream of thought was spearheaded in the early 1980s by Ian Hodder, formerly of Cambridge University and now in Stanford University (Fig. 1.8). He obtained the initial clues for these ideas from his ethnographic work among the cattle-keeping Nuba tribes of Sudan. This work brought in the important realization that various material culture items do not have mere survival value but simultaneously carry with them many symbolic connotations. Hodder's studies revealed how patterning in the Nuba material culture (burials, settlements, artefacts, etc.) is actually produced by rules prescribing purity, boundedness and categories. The title of his book, *Symbols in Action* (1982a), reporting this research captures well the new theme.

Fig. 1.8 Ian Hodder (1948–) of Stanford University, principal proponent of Interpretive Archaeology.

In the same year Ian Hodder brought out an edited volume entitled *Symbolic and Structural Archaeology* (1982b). The essays in this volume represent a strong reaction against the ecological, functionalist and adaptationist orientations of the New Archaeology. As such the appearance of this volume marked the beginning of post-processual archaeology. The innovative aspect of these studies concerned the emphasis on the symbolic dimensions of things that people make and use in daily life. In processual archaeology some arbitrariness is associated with symbol systems. Neither the use of a particular artefact class for symbolizing, e.g. social status, nor the choice of the symbol itself is fully accounted for. The studies included in this volume sought to overcome this difficulty by attempting to explain the non-arbitrary character of symbols. To give an example, the shape of prehistoric burials of a given region was seen appropriate, since it referred back to the earlier house form and thus carried with it evocative feelings. We are thus told that

> ... material items come to have symbolic meanings as a result both of their use in structured sets and of the associations of

> the objects themselves, but that the meanings vary with context. It is through these various mechanisms that material items and the constructed world come to represent society (Hodder 1982c: 9-10).

In subsequent years, Hodder developed this theme in many research papers and book-length publications. So too was the case with some of the younger British archaeologists including some of Hodder's own students. Thus, in the next two decades, a sizeable amount of literature appeared in print. And, predictably enough, as in the case of the New Archaeology, several sub-trends made their appearance in post-processeual or interpretive archaeology too. These may broadly be grouped into two kinds, i.e., those touching upon the epistemological dimensions of the discipline and the ones dealing with sociological aspects of the study of the past (Pinsky and Wylie 1989; Preucel 1991; Johnson 1999). The former includes such trends as Hodder's own contextual archaeology/approach, symbolic/semiotic archaeology, hermeneutical archaeology, phenomenological archaeology, cognitive archaeology, agency theory, etc. Tilley's essay on 'Archaeology as Socio-political Action in the Present' (1989) is a comprehensive statement about the sociological dimensions of the study of the past. A few general observations are in order about these soft or ideational trends.

First, just as the processual trends were in a way a re-enactment of the positivist thought that had become a dominant trend in many natural and social sciences in the middle of the last century, these soft approaches too were spurred both by mind-oriented perspectives that had come up in geography, anthropology and other disciplines and the 'anarchist' theory of knowledge that had cropped up in philosophy of science between the 1950s and

1970s. The 'anarchist' theory of knowledge was spearheaded by Paul Feyerabend (1988) and T.S. Kuhn (1962) who, while not denying the importance of a rational method in the investigation of empirical world, drew attention to the need to take note of the changes that come up in its standards from time to time. Post-processual trends were also a reflection of the return of 'Grand Theory', which tends to frame abstract and normative theories of human nature and conduct (Paddayya 1990: 20-43).

For methodological purposes, post-processual archaeology took inspiration from the writings of the 19th century German philosopher Wilhelm Dilthey and those of the British philosopher and historian R.G. Collingwood. While Collingwood advocated the procedure of imaginative re-enactment of the past in the historian's mind, Dilthey declared that we *explain* (erklären) nature but understand (*verstehen)* human culture. He therefore introduced hermeneutics (interpretation) as the special method of cultural sciences. Post-processual archaeology found in hermeneutics a handy tool and redefined archaeological record as text from which we need to extract meanings about the past. The issue now was not one of acquiring objective knowledge about the past but one of understanding human intentions and sentiments and the symbolism conveyed through human actions. Epistemology thus gave way to ontology (*zu den Sachen*, as the phenomenologist Husserl put it) and causality in the natural world to teleology. With these changes post-processual archaeology sought to demolish the dichotomies that the New Archaeology had raised between objectivity and subjectivity, society and individual, general and particular, and materialist and ideational worlds. In tune with these fundamental changes, many new terms such as individual, role, norm, action, meaning, evocation, mediation and context were introduced in the conceptual apparatus (Shanks and Hodder 1995).

Some of these perspectives have been employed with good results for studying the Neolithic and Bronze Age cultures of Britain. In his book *The Domestication of Europe*, Hodder sought to interpret the entire Neolithic sequence in Europe as the playing out of a long-term structure underlying architecture, burial practices and artefact styles. This structure, according to him, involved an opposition between the *domus* (house and domestic world) and the *agrios* (wild) and consisted of a set of rules or codes gradually spreading across Europe. Hodder also employed these interpretive approaches for reconstructing the Neolithic way of life in the Near East. Of particular importance are his prolonged investigations at the site of Çatalhöyük on the Konya plain of Anatolia (Turkey) and symbolic interpretations of figurines and paintings of humans, animals and birds. The themes depicted in these representations "include a social focus on memory construction and temporal depth, a symbolic focus on wild animals, violence, and death, and a central dominant role for humans in relation to the animal world" (Hodder 2007: 116). Hodder goes further and says that these themes were integral to the development of settled life and the domestication of plants and animals throughout West Asia.

In his two books *Rethinking the Neolithic* (1991) and *Time, Culture and Eternity* (2001), Julian Thomas adopted a hermeneutic approach and argued that the introduction of Neolithic way of life was not mere adoption of a Neolithic trait into the Mesolithic way of life. It was a wholesale transformation of social relations resulting from the adoption of an integrated cultural system. In his own words:

> Such a system has its purpose in not merely provision of sustenance, the biological reproduction of the community, but its social reproduction including the maintenance of power relations, knowledge and institutions. Owning a cow or an axe, living in a house, or burying one of one's kin in a particular way does not make a person Neolithic. It is the recognition of the symbolic potential of the elements to express a fundamental division of the universe into the wild and the tame which creates the Neolithic world (1991: 13).

Thomas considered at length the application of this symbolic or social approach to various aspects of the archaeological record, such as monuments, ceramics, lithics, and animal and plant materials. He also postulated that a great degree of variability existed between various areas in Neolithic Britain in terms of social and cultural practices.

Christopher Tilley's book *A Phenomenology of Landscape* (1994) made an attempt to introduce elements of humanistic geography into interpretation of landscapes of past societies. In the past, landscape had been regarded as mere physical compass or container for social action. The phenomenological perspective argues that space is much more than a silent container for action and that it cannot just be considered apart from events and activities that take place within it. Accordingly, Tilley treated landscape as a series of locales or sets of relational places linked by paths, movements and narratives. Thus, landscape in which a community is located is not a passive three-dimensional entity but is a cultural world which in turn shapes the human mind. The geographer Tuan (1976) called this attitude of mind geopiety.

Mark Edmonds' *Ancestral Geographies of the Neolithic* (1999) is another book which attempts to recapture the social world of the Neolithic groups of Britain during the 4th millennium BC. Relying upon evidence pertaining to the landscape and monuments located on it, Edmonds visualizes Neolithic Britain as a world shaped by kinship, ancestry and other forms of affiliation. The dead were a powerful presence in this world and distant times and places held a particular fascination to the people. These affiliations were brought into a sharp focus at the time of periodic gatherings at monuments, enclosures and monuments. At these gatherings, the community engaged in ancestral sites, exchange and other forms of ceremonial activity. It was through these routine as well as ritual experiences that the otherwise dispersed and fragmented communities not only strengthened their bonds with one another but also promoted their ties with the land and their past.

In a more recent book entitled *Ideas of Landscape* (2007), Matthew Johnson argues that, apart from the comparative, generalizing approaches to landscape advocated by processual and post-processual archaeologies, theory and practice of landscape archaeology could also benefit from the British tradition pioneered by W.S. Hoskins and other workers for dealing with landscapes of the historical periods. Johnson (2007: 183) describes it as "humanistic, particularistic, interested in *genius loci*, and closely implicated in the concerns of history", and traces its roots to English Romanticism of the 18th century with William Wordsworth as one of the key figures, as against phenomenology and hermeneutics invoked by post-processualists.

As to the sociological dimensions, Tilley's paper "Archaeology as Socio-political action in the present" (1989) has drawn attention to the need for fresh historiographical studies in archaeology, improvements in museum displays, heritage studies and public education, and fresh studies of the archaeological record to expose social and gender inequalities.

Thus, it is clear that post-processual archaeology is a set of diverse perspectives and encourages multiple approaches to the past. As stated by Hodder himself, "...post-processual archaeology is simply 'post'—... It involves diversity and lack of consensus. It is characterized by debate and uncertainty about fundamental issues that may have been rarely questioned before in archaeology. It is more an asking of questions than a provision of answers" (Hodder 1986: 170).

It is amazing to recall that more than 100 years ago Flinders Petrie, in his book *Methods and Aims in Archaeology* (1904), which may well be the first book-length account of the basic principles of archaeology, was already anticipating both the adaptationist and ideational goals of archaeology now formalized by the New Archaeology and subsequent developments. He also commented on the social relevance of the study of past. In a memorable statement, Petrie remarked that archeology is "the science which enquires into all the products and works of our own species, which shows what man has been doing in all ages and under all conditions, which reveal man's mind, his thoughts, his tastes and feelings" (1972: vii). Commenting on the place of archaeology in liberal education, he wrote:

> Archaeology—the knowledge of how man has acquired his present position and powers—is one of the widest studies... it is best fitted to open the mind and to produce that type of wide interests and toleration which is the highest result of education (1972: viii).

REFERENCES

Adams, R.M. 1965. *Land behind Baghdad: A History of Settlement on the Diyala Plains*. Chicago: University of Chicago Press.

——. 1966. *The Evolution of Urban Society: Early Mesopotamia and Prehispanic Mexico*. Chicago: Aldine.

Adams, R.M. & H.J. Nissen. 1972. *The Uruk Countryside: The Natural Setting of Urban Societies*. Chicago: University of Chicago Press.

Arnold III, P.J. 2003. Back to Basics: The Middle-Range Program as Pragmatic Archaeology. In T.L. VanPool and C.S. VanPool (eds.), *Essential Tensions in Archaeological Method and Theory*, pp. 55-66. Salt Lake City: University of Utah Press.

Bennett, J.W. 1943. Recent Developments in the Functional Interpretation of Archaeological Data. *American Antiquity* 9: 208-19.

Binford, L.R. 1962. Archaeology as Anthropology. *American Antiquity* 28: 217-25.

——. 1964. A Consideration of Archaeological Research Design. *American Antiqutiy* 29: 425-41.

——. 1965. Archaeological Systematics and the Study of Culture Process. *American Antiquity* 31: 203-10.

——. 1968a. Archaeological Perspectives. In S.R. Binford and L.R. Binford (eds.). *New Perspectives in Archaeology*, pp. 5-32. Chicago: Aldine.

——. 1968b. Post-Pleistocene Adaptations. In S.R. Binford and L.R. Binford (eds.), *New Perspectives in Archaeology*, pp. 313-41. Chicago: Aldine.

——. 1972a. *An Archaeological Perspective*. New York: Seminar Press.

——. 1972b. Contemporary Model Building: Paradigms and the Current State of Palaeolithic Research. In D.L. Clarke (ed.), *Models in Archaeology*, pp. 109-66. London: Methuen.

——. (ed.). 1977. *For Theory Building in Archaeology: Essays on Faunal Remains, Aquatic Resources, Spatial Analysis, and Systemic Modeling*. New York: Academic Press.

——. 1978. *Nunamiut Ethnoarchaeology*. New York: Academic Press.

——. 1980. Willow Smoke and Dogs' Tails: Hunter-gatherer Settlement Systems and Archaeological Site Formation. *American Antiquity* 45: 4-20.

——. 1981a. Behavioral Archaeology and the "Pompeii Premise". *Journal of Anthropological Research* 37: 195-208.

——. 1981b. *Bones: Ancient Men and Modern Myths*. New York: Academic Press.

——. 1983a. *Working at Archaeology*. New York: Academic Press.

——. 1983b. *In Pursuit of the Past: Decoding the Archaeological Record.* New York: Thames and Hudson.

——. 1986. In Pursuit of the Future. In D.J. Meltzer, D. Fowler and J.A. Sabloff (eds.), *American Archaeology: Past and Future*, pp. 459-79. Washington, D.C.: Smithsonian Institution Press.

——. 1989. *Debating Archaeology*. San Diego: Academic Press. Republished in 2009 in paperback edition, with a new preface, by Left Coast Press, Walnut Geek, California.

——. 2001. *Constructing Frames of Reference: An Analytical Method for Archaeological Theory Building Using Ethnographic and Environmental Data Sets.* Berkeley: University of California Press.

Binford, L.R. and S.R. Binford. 1966. A Preliminary Analysis of Functional Variability in the Mousterian of Levallois Facies. *American Anthropologist* 68: 238-95.

Binford, S.R. and L.R. Binford (eds.). 1968. *New Perspectives in Archaeology*. Chicago: Aldine. Republished as *Archaeology in Cultural Systems* in 2008. Chicago: Aldine Transaction.

——. 1969. Stone Tools and Human Behaviour. *Scientific American* 220: 92-101.

Blauberg, I.V., V.N. Sadovsky and E.G. Yudin. 1977. *Systems Theory: Philosophical and Methodological Problems.* Moscow: Progress

Publishers. Translated from Russian by S. Syrovattin and O. Germogenova.

Braidwood, R.J. 1974. The Iraq Jarmo Project. In G.R. Willey (ed.), *Archaeological Researches in Retrospect,* pp. 61-83. Cambridge (MA): Harvard University Press.

Brothwell, D. and E. Higgs (eds.). 1963. *Science in Archaeology: A Survey of Progress and Research.* London: Thames and Hudson.

Butzer, K.W. 1982. *Archaeology as Human Ecology: Method and Theory for a Contextual Approach.* Cambridge: Cambridge University Press.

Capra, Fritjof. 1997. *The Web of Life: A New Synthesis of Mind and Matter.* London: Harper Collins Publishers.

Chang, K.C. (ed.). 1968. *Settlement Archaeology.* Palo Alto: National Press Books.

Childe, V.G. 1935. Changing Methods and Aims in Prehistory: Presidential Address. *Proceedings of the Prehistoric Society* 1: 1-15.

——. 1936. *Man Makes Himself.* London: Watts and Co.

——. 1942. *What Happened in History.* New York: Penguin.

——. 1956. *Piecing Together the Past: The Interpretation of Archaeological Data.* London: Routledge and Kegan Paul.

Clark, J.G.D. 1960. *Archaeology and Society: Reconstructing the Past.* London: Methuen. First published in 1939.

Clarke, D.L. 1962. Matrix Analysis and Archaeology with Particular Reference to British Beaker Pottery. *Proceedings of the Prehistoric Society* 15: 371-82.

——. 1968. *Analytical Archaeology.* London: Methuen.

——. 1972. A Provisional Model of an Iron Age Society and Its Settlement System. In D.L. Clarke (ed.), *Models in Archaeology,* pp. 801-69. London: Methuen.

——. 1973. Archaeology: The Loss of Innocence. *Antiquity* 47: 6-18.

——. 1978. *Mesolithic Europe: The Economic Basis.* London: Duckworth.

Copi, I.M. and J.A. Gould (eds.). 1972. *Readings on Logic*. New York: Macmillan.

Daniel, Glyn E. 1967. *The Origins and Growth of Archaeology.* Harmondsworth: Penguin.

——. 1975. *150 Years of Archaeology*. London: Duckworth.

DeVore, I. 1968. Comments. In S.R. Binford and L.R. Binford (eds.), *New Perspectives in Archaeology,* pp. 346-47. Chicago: Aldine.

Earle, T.K. 1991. Toward a Behavioral Archaeology. In R.W. Preucel (ed.), *Processual and Postprocessual Archaeologies*, pp. 83-95. Carbondale: Southern Illinois University Press.

Edmonds, Mark. 1999. *Ancestral Geographies of the Neolithic: Landscape, Monuments and Memory.* London: Routledge.

Emery, F.E. (ed.). 1969. *Systems Thinking: Selected Readings*. Harmondsworth: Penguin.

Feyerabend, Paul A. 1988. *Against Method.* Second Edition. London: Verso.

Flannery, K.V. (ed.). 1976. *The Early Mesoamerican Village*. New York: Academic.

——. 1986. (ed.). *Guila Naquitz: Archaic Foraging and Early Agriculture in Oaxaca, Mexico*. Orlando: Academic.

——. 2006. On the Resilience of Anthropological Archaeology. *Annual Review of Anthropology* 35: 1-13.

Gamble, C. 1999. Lewis Binford. In Tim Murray (ed.), *Encyclopedia of Archaeology—The Great Archaeologists.* Volume II, pp. 811-34. Santa Barbara, California: ABC-CLIO.

Griffin, J.B. 1985. An Individual's Participation in American Archaeology. *Annual Review of Anthropology* 14: 1-23.

Hahn, H., O. Neurath and R. Carnap. 1929. *Wissenschaftliche Weltauffassung: Der Wiener Kreis*. Translated and published as *The Scientific Conception of the World: The Vienna Circle* in 1973. Dordrecht: Reidel Publishing Company.

Heisenberg, W. 1952. *Philosophical Problems of Nuclear Science*. London: Faber and Faber.

Hempel, C.G. 1965. *Aspects of Scientific Explanation and Other Essays in the Philosophy of Science.* New York: Free Press.

Hodder, Ian. 1982a. *Symbols in Action: Ethnoarchaeological Studies of Material Culture.* Cambridge: Cambridge University Press.

——. (ed.). 1982b. *Symbolic and Structural Archaeology.* Cambridge: Cambridge University Press.

——. 1982c. Theoretical Archaeology: A Reactionary View. In Ian Hodder (ed.), *Symbolic and Structural Archaeology*, pp. 1-16. Cambridge: Cambridge University Press.

——. 1986. *Reading the Past: Current Approaches to Interpretation in Archaeology.* Cambridge: Cambridge University Press.

——. 1990. *The Domestication of Europe.* Oxford: Basil Blackwell.

——. 2007. Çatalhöyük in the Context of the Middle Eastern Neolithic. *The Annual Review of Anthropology* 36: 105-20.

——. 2011. Human-thing Entanglement: Towards an Integrated Archaeological Perspective. *Journal of the Royal Anthropological Institute* (N.S.) 17: 154-77.

Johnson, A.L. (ed.). 2004. *Processual Archaeology: Exploring Analytical Strategies, Frames of Reference and Culture Process.* West Port (CT): Praeger.

Johnson, M. 1999. *Archaeological Theory: An Introduction.* Malden (Ma): Blackwell Publishing.

——. 2007. *Ideas of Landscape.* Oxford: Blackwell Publishing.

Jones, Andrew. 2002. *Archaeological Theory and Scientific Practice.* Cambridge: Cambridge University Press.

Knapp, A.B. (ed.). 1992. *Archaeology, Annales and Ethnohistory.* Cambridge: Cambridge University Press.

Kress, R.M. 1970. *Social Science and the Idea of Process.* Urbana: University of Illinois Press.

Kuhn, T.S. 1962. *The Structure of Scientific Revolutions.* Chicago: University of Chicago Press. Revised edition in 1970.

——. 1977. *The Essential Tension: Selected Studies in Scientific Tradition and Change.* Chicago: University of Chicago Press.

Leone, M.P. (ed.). 1972. *Contemporary Archaeology: A Guide to Theory and Contributions*. Carbondale: Southern Illinois University Press.

Leone, M.P., P.B. Potter and P.A. Shackel. 1987. Toward a Critical Archaeology. *Current Anthropology* 28: 283-302.

MacNeish, R.S., M.L. Fowler, A.G. Cook, F.A. Peterson and J.A. Neely. *The Prehistory of the Tehuacan Valley, Volume 5: Excavations and Reconnaissance.* Austin: University of Texas Press.

Mandelbaum, M. 1977. *The Anatomy of Historical Knowledge.* Baltimore: John Hopkins University Press.

Martin, Paul S. 1972. The Revolution in Archaeology. In M.P. Leone (ed.), *Contemporary Archaeology: A Guide to Theory and Contributions,* pp. 5-12. Carbondale: Southern Illinois University Press.

Martindale, D. 1961. *The Nature and Types of Social Theory*. London: Routledge and Kegan Paul.

Maschner, H.D.G. (ed.). 1996. *Darwinian Archaeologies*. New York: Plenum.

Meggers, B.J. (ed.). 1968. *Anthropological Archaeology in the Americas*. Washington, D.C.: Anthropological Society of Washington.

Meltzer, D.J. 1979. Paradigms and the Nature of Change in American Archaeology. *American Antiquity* 44: 644-57.

——. 2011. *Lewis Roberts Binford 1931-2011: A Biographical Memoir*. Washington, D.C.: National Academy of Sciences.

Neurath, O., R. Carnap and C. Morris (eds.). 1955. *International Encyclopaedia of Unified Science,* Volume 1. Chicago: University of Chicago Press.

O'Brien, M.J. and R.L. Lyman. 2000. *Applying Evolutionary Archaeology: A Systematic Approach*. New York: Kluwer Academic.

O'Brien, M.J., R.L. Lyman and M.B. Schiffer. 2005. *Archaeology as a Process: Processualism and its Progeny*. Salt Lake City: University of Utah Press.

Odum, Eugene P. 1963. *Ecology.* New York: Holt, Reinehart and Winston.

——. 1971. *Fundamentals of Ecology.* Philadelphia: W.B. Saunders Company.

Paddayya, K. 1983. Myths about the New Archaeology. *Saeculum* 34: 70-104.

——. 1990. *The New Archaeology and Aftermath: A View from Outside the Anglo-American World.* Pune: Ravish Publishers.

Patrik, L.E. 1985. Is There an Archaeological Record? In M.B. Schiffer (ed.), *Advances in Archaeological Method and Theory* 8, pp. 27-62. New York: Academic Press.

Petrie, W. Flinders. 1972. *Methods and Aims in Archaeology.* New York: Benjamin Blom. Originally published in 1904.

Piggott, S. 1959. *Approach to Archaeology.* Harmondsworth: Penguin.

Pinsky, V. and A. Wylie (eds.). 1989.*Critical Traditions in Contemporary Archaeology.* Cambridge: Cambridge University Press.

Popper, K.R. 1980. *The Logic of Scientific Discovery.* London: Hutchinson.

Preucel, R.W. (ed.). 1991. *Processual and Post-processual Archaeologies: Multiple Ways of Knowing the Past.* Carbondale (Illinois): Southern Illinois University Press.

Preucel, R.W. and Ian Hodder (eds.). 1996.*Contemporary Archaeology in Theory: A Reader.* Blackwell Publishing.

Renfrew, C. 1994. Towards a Cognitive Archaeology. In C. Renfrew and E.B.W. Zubrow (eds.), *The Ancient Mind: Elements of Cognitive Archaeology,* pp. 3-12. Cambridge: Cambridge University Press.

Russell, Bertrand. 1976. *The Problems of Philosophy.* Oxford: Oxford University Press. Originally published in 1912.

Schiffer, M.B. 1976. *Behavioural Archaeology.* New York: Academic.

——. 1987. *Formation Processes of the Archaeological Record.* Albuquerque: University of New Mexico Press.

——. 1995. *Behavioral Archaeology: First Principles.* Salt Lake City: University of Utah Press.

Segraves, B.A. 1974. Ecological Generalization and Structural Transformation of Socio-Cultural Systems. *American Anthropologist* 76: 530-32.

Shanks, M. and I. Hodder. 1995. Processual, Post-processual and Interpretive Archaeologies. In I. Hodder *et al.* (eds.), *Interpreting Archaeology: Finding Meaning in the Past,* pp. 3-29. London: Routledge.

Snow, C.P. 1969. *The Two Cultures: A Second Look.* Cambridge: Cambridge University Press. First published in 1959.

Spriggs, M. (ed.). 1984. *Marxist Perspectives in Archaeology.* Cambridge: Cambridge University Press.

Steward, J. 1955. *Theory of Culture Change: The Methodology of Multilinear Evolution.* Urbana: University of Illinois Press.

Stickel, G.E. and Chartkoff, J.L. 1973. The Nature of Scientific Laws and Their Relation to Law-building in Archaeology. In C. Renfrew (ed.). *The Explanation of Culture Change: Models in Prehistory,* pp. 663-71. London: Duckworth.

Taylor, Meadows. 1989. *The Story of My Life.* London: Zwan Publications. Originally published in 1878.

Taylor, W.W. 1948. *A Study of Archaeology.* Memoir No. 69. Washington, D.C.: American Anthropological Association. Reprinted in 1983 by Southern Illinois University, Carbondale.

Thomas, Julian. 1991. *Rethinking the Neolithic.* Cambridge: Cambridge University Press.

——. 1996. *Time, Culture and Identity: An Interpretive Archaeology.* London: Routledge.

Thomsen, C.J. 1848. a) A Cursory View of the Monuments and Antiquities of the North; b) Objects of the Heathen Period; c) Of the Different Periods to which Heathen Antiquities May Be Referred. In *Guide to Northern Archaeology*, translated and edited by the Earl of Ellesmore. London: James-Bain. Originally published in Danish in 1836 as *Ledetraad til*

Nordisk Oldkindighed by the Royal Society of Northern Antiquities, Copenhagen.

Tilley, Christopher. 1989. Archaeology as Sociopolitical Action in the Present. In V. Pinsky and A. Wylie (eds.), *Critical Traditions in Contemporary Archaeology: Essays in the Philosophy, History and Sociopolitics of Archaeology*, pp. 104-16. Cambridge: Cambridge University Press.

—— (ed.). 1993. *Interpretative Archaeology*. Oxford: Berg Publications.

Trigger, Bruce. 1989. *A History of Archaeological Thought*. Cambridge: Cambridge University Press.

Tuan, Yi-fu. 1976. Geopiety: A Theme in Man's Attachment to Nature and Place. In D. Lowenthal and M.J. Bowden (eds.), *Geographies of the Mind: Essays in Historical Geosophy in Honor of John Kirtland Wright*, pp. 11-39. New York: Oxford University Press.

Watson, P.J., S.A. LeBlanc and C. Redman. 1971. *Explanation in Archaeology: An Explicitly Scientific Approach*. New York: Columbia University Press.

Watson, R.A. 1991. What the New Archaeology Has Achieved. *Current Anthropology* 32: 279-91.

Wheeler, R.E.M. 1949. Archaeological Fieldwork in India: Planning Ahead. *Ancient India* 5: 4-11.

White, L.A. 1959. *The Evolution of Culture: The Development of Civilization to the Fall of Rome*. New York: McGraw-Hill.

Willey, G.R. 1953. *Prehistoric Settlement Patterns in the Viru Valley, Peru*. Bulletin No. 155. Washington, D.C.: Bureau of American Ethnology.

Willey, G.R. and P. Phillips. 1958. *Method and Theory in American Archaeology*. Chicago: University of Chicago Press.

Willey, G.R. and J.A. Sabloff. 1980. *A History of American Archaeology*. Second edition. San Francisco: W.H. Freeman & Co.

Wilson, E.O. 1999. *Consilience: Unity of Knowledge*. New York: Vintage Publications.

Winters, H.D. 1969. *The Riverton Culture: A Second Millennium Occupation in the Central Wabash Valley*. Report No. 13. Springfield: Illinois State Museum.

Wylie, M.A. 1981. *Positivism and the New Archaeology*. Ann Arbor: University Microfilms.

——. 2002. *Thinking from Things: Essays in the Philosophy of Archaeology.* Chicago: University of Chicago Press.

CHAPTER II

Theoretical Perspectives in Indian Archaeology

INTRODUCTION

In this chapter, we shall review the use of theoretical perspectives in Indian archaeology. The establishment of The Asiatic Society in Kolkata by Sir William Jones in 1784 placed the antiquarian studies in India on an institutionalized footing. The following century witnessed many pioneering contributions made by Colin Mackenzie, James Prinsep, James Fergusson, Meadows Taylor, Alexander Cunningham and Robert Bruce Foote. These studies led to the emergence of epigraphy, numismatics, art and architecture, prehistory, protohistory and historical archaeology as distinct branches. In the first quarter of the 20th century, remains of a full-fledged Bronze Age Civilization were uncovered in the Indus basin. Till Independence, archaeological investigations were exclusively in the hands of the Archaeological Survey of India and some princely states such as Mysore, Baroda and Hyderabad.

After Independence, archaeology was introduced as part of the curriculum of universities, which also initiated detailed field investigations in various parts of the country. The combined efforts of government departments and universities over the last six decades have provided a much more comprehensive picture of various phases of the country's past (for details, see Sankalia 1962, 1977a, 1979; Fairservis 1971; Agrawal 1982; Thapar 1985; Allchin and Allchin 1982, 1997; Dhavalikar 1997, 1999; Kennedy 2000; Agrawal and Kharakwal 2002, 2003; Mate 2005; Chakrabarti 2006). Suffice it to say that the Stone Age occupation has now been proved to have an antiquity of 1.5 million years and that it consists of Lower, Middle and Upper Palaeolithic phases and the Mesolithic, all securely dated by means of absolute dating techniques. The reconstruction of lifeways of these phases is based on the excavation of *in situ* cultural horizons and use of ethnographic analogies. Advances in protohistory include the discovery of over 1000 Harappan sites east of the Indus basin; identification of over a dozen early agro-pastoral culture complexes; and excavation of Iron Age occupation sites. Historical and medieval archaeology too witnessed important developments, including major excavations. The use of earth, biological and physical sciences also led to a more comprehensive understanding of environmental as well as cultural dimensions of the country's archaeological record.

As regards theory use in Indian archaeology, the story is again long but its history is brief. In his book *The Personality of India* (1956), B. Subbarao initiated what is called the anthropogeographical approach in Indian archaeology (Fig. 2.1). Although rarely cited in the literature, Allchin published in 1961 a short but the first ever truly historiographical account of Indian archaeology. In this article, Allchin went beyond the narration of events and instead focused attention on the intellectual environment of the four main periods in the development of Indian archaeology, viz., the period up to 1850; Cunningham

Fig. 2.1 Bendapudi Subbarao (1923–1962), Founder-Head of the Department of Archaeology at the M.S. University of Vadodara and of *The Personality of India* (1956) fame.

period; Marshall period; and Wheeler period and thereafter. Right from the 18th century, views have been expressed about the nature and origins of cultural items, practices and institutions. Egyptian or Chinese origin of cave architecture at Elephanta; Greek origin of the Buddha image of the Gandhara school; Sir William Jones's postulation of an Indo-European family of languages; derivation of the Stone Age cultures from Western Europe or West Asia; and West Asiatic origins of early food-producing cultures are well-known examples. These and other examples have been dealt with by Subbarao (1958), Chakrabarti (1989) and other writers.

While these views and interpretations no doubt enlivened the lengthy reports on field investigation of sites and monuments, they were not aimed at providing any definite conceptual or methodological strategies to deal with archaeological record itself. As such these views, while they no doubt helped link up various kinds of data or content of archaeology, do not touch upon the larger epistemological dimensions, i.e., archaeology as a knowledge-seeking discipline. In short, the difference is between speculative and analytic trends in philosophy of history (Lemon 2003). So, without altogether ignoring their place in the development of archaeology, we keep them in abeyance in our discussions of theory use in the analytic sense.

BEGINNINGS OF THEORETICAL DEBATES

Regular theory implies formulation of definite conceptual and methodological perspectives, which enable archaeologists to actually operate with the archeological record at various levels of study—its character and mode of occurrence; methods for its exploration and excavation; use of interpretative perspectives; and the short- or long-term benefits of the study of the past to the society at large. This is theory in its full-fledged epistemological and sociological senses. Theory thus directs practice and is more or less synonymous with Thomas Kuhn's (1962: x) definition of paradigm "as a universally recognized scientific achievement that for a time provides model problems and solutions to a community of practitioners."

Theory in the Kuhnian sense of research paradigms grappling with model problems and solutions came up in Indian archaeology in the 60s and 70s of the last century. It is for all practical purposes an outgrowth of the emergence of the New Archaeology in the Anglo-American world, as represented by the writings of Lewis Binford from America and David Clarke from England. S.C. Malik's book *Indian Civilization—The Formative Period* (1968; see also 1975) represents the first wave of influence of these new ideas (Fig. 2.2). Malik's affiliation with the Department of Anthropology at Chicago University between 1963 and 1965 as a Fulbright-Smith-Mundt scholar helped him breathe the anthropological spirit of American archaeology. His stay coincided with the new and rebellious ideas that were being formulated there by Lewis Binford. Binford's two manifesto-making articles entitled "Archaeology as Anthropology" (1962) and "A

Fig. 2.2 Subash C. Malik (1932–) delivering the H.D. Sankalia memorial lecture at the Annual Conference of Indian Society for Prehistoric and Quaternary Studies held at Vadodara in November 2012.

Consideration of Archaeological Research Design" (1964) appeared in print and were already making waves. It was but inevitable that Malik came under the spell of these new ideas emphasizing the importance of both conceptual clarifications and identification of past cultural processes. Malik (1968: xii) himself admits that he was "greatly influenced by the ideas and orientation of Binford and others and thanked all of them for widening my horizons in both archaeology and anthropology". On his return to India, he developed these ideas further as a Senior Fellow of the Centre of Advanced Study in Simla and his book *Indian Civilization—The Formative Period* grew out of this research.

Malik's book aimed "to suggest a reorientation of the research goals" in Indian archaeology, with emphasis on functional approaches and socio-cultural processes (1968: 92-3). Unfortunately, as it happened earlier in American archaeology in the case of Walter Taylor's book *A Study of Archaeology* (1948), workers in Indian archaeology failed to grasp the overall significance of Malik's new propositions. I think the reason for this dull response was threefold. First, the ideas were good but the context or time for their acceptance was not ripe; in the 1950s and 1960s, archaeologists in India were still preoccupied with the foundation work of establishing regional culture-sequences. Secondly, he did not have any regular institutional affiliation that could have helped give a stamp of authority to his views. Thirdly, the poor response was also due to the fact that Malik was far from a practising archaeologist and his first-hand familiarity with the archaeological record was limited to the discovery of a few Stone Age sites of secondary context in the Konkan region (Malik 1965).

H.D. Sankalia's two lectures at the Ethnographic and Folk Culture Society in Lucknow in 1974 served as the effective beginning of the influence of the New Archaeology in the country (Fig. 2.3). In these lectures Sankalia made a detailed review of the two major books that appeared in 1968, viz., D.L. Clarke's *Analytical Archaeology* and *New Perspectives in Archaeology* edited by Sally and Lewis Binford. He also pointed out how these new ideas could be

Fig. 2.3 Hasmukh Dhirajlal Sankalia (1908–1989), Founder-Head of the Department of Archaeology at the Deccan College, Pune.

used with profit in Indian prehistoric and protohistoric studies. Sankalia's lectures were published in 1977 as a book entitled *New Archaeology: Its Scope and Application to India* (Sankalia 1977b). In 1985, the Department of Ancient Indian History, Culture and Archaeology of Banaras Hindu University published two small but useful books. In one of these books Bruce Trigger, probably irked by the New Archaeology's call for treating archaeology as anthropology, put forward arguments in favour of archaeology as a historical science (Trigger 1985). In the second book entitled *Models, Paradigms and the New Archaeology,* Shivaji Singh briefly examined the tenets of the New Archaeology and also emphasized the role of models (Singh 1985).

Sankalia's book and personal exhortations to his colleagues and students soon created much interest in these new ideas coming from the Anglo-American world. My own interest in theoretical archaeology commenced with a review of Sankalia's book just mentioned above (Paddayya 1978). I pursued this interest further, including the completion of a few courses in philosophy of science, and published several papers on this topic subsequently (Paddayya 1980, 1981, 1982a, 1983, 1985, 1986, 1989). The New Arcaheology formulations took a firm shape in India with the All-India Refresher Course in the New Archaeology, which M.K. Dhavalikar organized at the Deccan College, Pune, in May-June 1986. Lewis Binford himself was one of the principal resource persons and gave several inspiring lectures (Paddayya 2012a). These and his informal discussions with the participants helped spread the new concepts and methods to other places in India as well.

The end of the decade saw the publication of two other books on this topic. D.K. Chakrabarti's book *Theoretical Issues in Indian Archaeology* (1989) basically focused on the role of geographical factors, diffusion of culture, biased racial interpretations of the

European workers, and such other general issues, but without any specific reference to actual operational strategies required for dealing with the archaeological record itself. In my book *The New Archaeology and Aftermath: A View from Outside the Anglo-American World* (1990), I drew attention to the departures made by the New Archaeology and soft or interpretive approaches in the conceptual and methodological domains and their usefulness in the investigation of archaeological record pertaining to pre- and protohistoric cultures in India. I also commented briefly on the social relevance and other aspects of the study of the past.

During the last two decades, several other contributions in the form of research papers have appeared. I have myself published two additional papers giving the main developments in Indian archaeology since the establishment of the Asiatic Society in Kolkata and the theoretical approaches associated with these developments (Paddayya 1995, 2002a). I have also pointed out the relevance of processual and post-processual approaches in the context of Indian archaeology. Further, in 1997, a national-level seminar was held at the Deccan College on the topic of formation processes and their significance in Indian archaeology (Paddayya, Jhaldiyal and Deo 2007). In 2002, Dorian Fuller and Nicole Boivin (Fuller and Boivin 2002; Boivin and Fuller 2002) presented their own reviews of the place of processual and post-processual trends in Indian archaeology. Focussing attention on the contributions of H.D. Sankalia at the Deccan College, Sheena Panja argued that post-Independence archaeology sought the services of both biological and physical sciences and began to carve an independent path for itself (Panja 2002). Indrani Chattopadhyaya (2002) examined the relevance of symbolic trends in the study of the Mesolithic phase. Umesh

Chattopadhyaya (2000: 177) underscored the need "to develop fundamental research in archaeology, incorporating philosophical and sociological perspectives and elaborating archaeology's relevance in the contemporary world."

During the last five or six years, a few more writings have appeared on this topic. While she does not oppose the use of the New Archaeology's perspectives, Nayanjot Lahiri (2006) correctly pointed out that there is still tremendous scope for culture history approach in Indian archaeology with particular reference to the building up of regional stratigraphical and chronological frameworks. In a very interesting paper entitled "People's Archaeology and Archaeology for the People", Shrimali (2009) deplored that after Independence Indian archaeology laid too much emphasis on protohistoric investigations and neglected historical and medieval archaeology. He emphasized the use of textual and inscriptional data to complement archaeological record. He also called for more field investigations in archaeology and people-oriented publications. In two of his publications Ajay Pratap (2009a, b), while admitting the importance of processual perspectives, stated that there was a greater need for a historical approach in ethnoarchaeological investigations, including the use of contextual analogy advocated by post-processual archaeology.

The above citations do not permit one to conclude that theoretical discussions are widespread in Indian archaeology. On the contrary, the general awareness of the relevance of theory is very limited. The responses of workers range from lukewarm attitude to downright cynicism. For example, Dilip Chakrabarti (2001: 1192) called these theoretical debates "pleasant noises". In a job-interview I faced many years ago at the Deccan College itself, one of the experts likened the debates about theoretical perspectives in archaeology to changes in the shapes of bottoms of men's trousers—from loose-pipes to bell-bottoms to drain-pipes. This negative attitude becomes all the more glaring when one considers the loose usage of various terms and concepts ranging from type and assemblage to hypothesis and causality. Field investigations are still conducted mostly without reference to a specific plan, leading only to vast and mindless accumulations of antiquarian remains. David Clarke's characterization of archaeology as "an undisciplined empirical discipline" seems to hold good in our case too. There is however a silver lining! There are some case studies in Indian archaeology which benefited from the use of more recent theoretical perspectives. We shall now examine them briefly; one hopes that their number will increase considerably in the years to come.

IMPACT OF THE NEW ARCHAEOLOGY

Before considering the case studies involving the impact of the New Archaeology, let us recapitulate its principal tenets, as developed by Binford and Clarke:

1. Going beyond the historian's goals of reconstructing site and regional culture-sequences, Binford advocated the anthropological goals of recognizing and explaining cultural similarities and differences across time and space.
2. Rising above the prevailing big-site approach in field archaeology, Binford laid emphasis on the need to examine the archaeological record in its regional and inter-regional contexts.
3. Going beyond the descriptive and classificatory dimensions of the archaeological record, the New Archaeology treated it as the product of human behaviour and thereby provided scope for making important statements about past lifeways.

4. This in turn led to major conceptual changes—particularly propositions such as cultures as systemic wholes and as means of human adaptation; and importance of generalizations for abstracting interrelationships among culture components.
5. All these ideas in turn entailed some major changes or innovations in field archaeology: a) regional orientation to the archaeological record; b) use of sampling and other methods for dealing with the field record; and c) raising hypotheses and testing them to unravel past cultural processes.

As I mentioned in the previous lecture, it is true that some of the above propositions could be found as isolated statements in the writings of some of the earlier Anglo-American archaeologists, such as Gordon Childe, Grahame Clark and James Bennett. But one must bear in mind that the newness of New Archaeology lies in pooling these ideas together and framing them into a regular manifesto. More importantly, the New Archaeology also put forward operational strategies for tackling the archaeological record, both in the field and in the laboratory.

Stone Age Studies

Prehistoric studies in India have a history of 150 years and commenced within a few years after their birth in Europe. Bruce Foote's discoveries of Palaeolithic sites in south India and Archibald Carlylle's recovery of microlithic artefacts from rock shelters in the Kaimur hills of Mirzapur area laid firm foundations for Stone Age studies in the second half of the 19th century (see Paddayya 2009, 2011: 11-14). Cammiade and Burkitt's work in the Kurnool area in 1930 led to the reconstruction of a four-phase culture sequence (series I to IV, corresponding to Early, Middle and Upper Palaeolithic, and Mesolithic stages) based on stratigraphical and typo-technological grounds, with palaeoclimatic implications. This formed the first paradigm in Indian Stone Age prehistory. The later field studies of Zeuner and Sankalia in western India and those of De Terra and Paterson in the Soan Valley of northwest India added further support to this paradigm. Thanks particularly to the work of Sankalia and his associates at the Deccan College, this emerged as a dominant paradigm by the 1970s (Sankalia 1974).

However, by the mid-70s some reactions began to build up against this paradigm. While the fundamental contributions made by this paradigm to the recognition of a basic culture-sequence and identification of relative stratigraphical/chronological positions and characteristic features of various cultural phases were no doubt widely appreciated, doubts began to be raised about the cultural interpretations made on the basis of stone-tool assemblages picked up at random from secondary contexts, such as river gravels and silts. Reacting against the preoccupation of workers with the collection and description of stone tools, Mortimer Wheeler (1960: 34, 63) dubbed the whole study as a matter of "Stones" and "More Stones". The need to rise above descriptive studies was felt more keenly with the introduction of the New Archaeology's propositions into the country. Emphasis now began to be laid on the discovery of primary sites preserving *in situ* Stone Age cultural material and also on the need for a regional approach to the archaeological record. A need was also felt to involve earth and biological sciences for reconstructing past environmental settings and for supplementing the evidence of archaeological record with ethnographic and experimental analogies (Paddayya 1979; Allchin 1994; Mohanty and Mishra

2002). These strategies are part of the settlement system perspective advocated by the New Archaeology. Thus, a new paradigm appeared in Indian prehistory (Paddayya 1978).

Against this background, university and government departments undertook, in collaboration with foreign institutions in some cases, fresh field studies covering both Palaeolithic and Mesolithic sites in many regions during the last three decades. These areas include the Kortallayar basin of Tamil Nadu, Kurnool and Cuddapah basins of Andhra Pradesh, Pravara and Upper Bhima valleys in Maharashtra, Kaladgi and Bhima basins of lower Deccan (north Karnataka), middle Ganga valley, Chotanagpur hills, western Rajasthan, and Orsang and other valleys of Gujarat (for general reviews, see Sankalia 1977a; Misra 1987a, 1989, 2002; Murty 1979; Paddayya 1984, 2008a; Mishra 1995; 2008a: Misra and Pal 1997, 2002; Pappu 2001; Dennell 2009).

As part of this fresh phase of field research, excavations were conducted at many Palaeolithic sites. These include cave and open air sites in the Kurnool area of Andhra Pradesh; Attirampakkam in Tamil Nadu; Anagwadi, Lakhmapur, Hunsgi, Yediyapur and Isampur in Karnataka; Chirki-Nevasa, Patne, Bori and Morgaon in Maharashtra; Bhimbetka, Samnapur, Nakjhar Khurd, Baghor and other sites in Central India; Paisra in Bihar; and Singi Talav and 16 R Dune site near Didwana in Rajasthan. The Acheulian sites at Attirampakkam and Isampur have been dated to 1.5 and 1.2 million years, respectively, by means of absolute dating methods (Pappu *et al.* 2002). The Middle Palaeolithic levels at 16 R dune site at Didwana are dated to 0.2 million years; those at Jwalapuram Locality 3, associated with volcanic tuff, in the Jurreru Valley of Kurnool are dated to 75,000 years (Petraglia *et al.* 2007). The Upper Palaeolithic began about 40,000 years ago. Likewise, excavations and other field investigations were conducted at the Mesolithic sites of Bagor and Tilwara in Rajasthan, Sanganakallu in Karnataka, Bhimbetka in central India; and Mahadaha, Damdama and Sarai Nahar Rai in the Ganga valley. Excavations at a rock shelter locality in the Jurreru Valley of Kurnool area take back the antiquity of blade-based microlithic tools to 34,000 BP (Clarkson *et al.* 2009). At Mehtakheri in central India, microlithic traditions have been dated to 48,000 years BP (Mishra, Chauhan and Singhvi 2009).

In all these Palaeolithic and Mesolithic excavations, occupation debris was exposed carefully in horizontal levels and also all cultural materials were point-plotted and photo-documented. In some of these cases, archaeological investigations were supplemented by ethnographic and experimental analogies. All these studies were influenced, directly or otherwise, by the New Archaeology's larger goal of reconstructing Stone Age adaptational processes. Without meaning to give an exhaustive list, I would like to illustrate this point with reference to the following case studies with which I have some degree of personal acquaintance.

A major development in the Stone Age research of post-Independence period relates to V.N. Misra's prolonged field investigations including systematic excavations in central India and Rajasthan (Misra 1973, 1978, 1985, 1987b, 1989, 1995). His excavations for several seasons in the caves of Bhimbetka complex exposed a full-fledged Stone Age sequence (from late Acheulian to the Mesolithic) with sealed cultural levels, representing various stages in the development of technology and typology. This work apart, Misra documented the hunting and food-gathering activities of the Gond groups living in the area. This ethnographic research gave many helpful clues about the settlement and subsistence aspects of Stone Age communities (Misra 1990; Nagar and Mishra 1993). In central India, Acheulian sites in primary context were also found at Lalitpur in Bundelkhand district (Singh 1965) and as a large cluster in Raisen district (Jacobson 1985).

Another major and long-term project completed by Misra concerns Rajasthan, more particularly its arid western part. His two initial excavations at the Mesolithic sites of Bagor and Tilwara in Nagor district exposed full-fledged settlement sites showing how a hunting-gathering community slowly acquired traits like settled life, domestic animals and even metal objects by interacting first with local food-producing cultures of the Chalcolithic phase and then with the Harappan culture itself. This is a clear example of the process of acculturation. The work of Misra and his team in the arid, dune-studded western Rajasthan made it possible to reconstruct the palaeoenvironmental history, showing how the area, once fed by regular streams, started experiencing aridity leading to the formation of sand-dunes. This work also showed how the Stone Age groups adapted themselves to these climatic changes; human occupation in this area stretched right from the Lower Palaeolithic stage to the Mesolithic phase (Misra 1987b, 1995).

Ajithprasad (2007) discovered a cluster of over 40 Acheulian sites in a small area of 300 km^2 lying in the middle reaches of the river Orsang in Gujarat. He noted that the majority of these sites are of a primary context, located either in the foothill zone of hill-ridges or along the courses of small feeder-streams. In a few cases, groups of sites were found around natural depressions measuring up to 100 m in diameter and preserving water till February or March. The use of seventy types of wild plant foods was noted in the area. These data hold clues for settlement system reconstructions.

In northern Deccan, with the culture-sequence recognized at Nevasa by Sankalia in 1956 serving as the basis, several primary sites have been investigated. These include the Acheulian sites at Chirki-Nevasa in the Pravara Valley (Corvinus 1981, 1983), and Bori and Morgaon in the upper Bhima Valley (Mishra *et al.* 2009). Sali's excavation at Patne exposed a detailed culture-sequence covering the Middle and Upper Palaeolithic and Mesolithic cultures (Sali 1989).

Coming further south, a noteworthy example is provided by M.L.K. Murty's prolonged field investigations spanning three decades and more in the Erramalai and Nallamalai ranges of the Eastern Ghats running through southwestern Andhra Pradesh. He discovered well-developed blade-and-burin assemblages in the Ralllakalva basin of Chittoor district and these findings firmly established the existence of a true Upper Palaeolithic phase in India (Murty 1968). His subsequent work involved intensive explorations in the whole region and detailed excavations in the caves of Kurnool area, particularly Billa Surgam and Muchchatla Chintamanu Gavi (Murty 1974). All these field studies led to the discovery of many Stone Age sites ranging from the Lower Palaeolithic to the Mesolithic. Unlike the earlier field studies in India, which primarily dealt with secondary occurrences of artefacts, Murty identified a large number of *in situ* or primary context sites. These occurred in varied topographical contexts, such as sandy beds of seasonal streams, scatters on river terraces, clusters on flat rock surfaces along streams, and caves and rockshelters. In addition to these meticulous field studies, Murty undertook detailed ethnoarchaeological studies of various living hunting-gathering and fishing societies of the area, more particularly the Chenchu, Boya, Yerukala, Yanadi and Jalari communities.

Based on these field studies, Murty attempted a reconstruction of the settlement and subsistence behaviour of the Stone Age communities (Murty 1981, 1985). Two or three of his observations are worth citing. First, in the Acheulian stage hominin occupation took place mostly in the shallow valleys enclosed by hills and probably covered with open vegetation of the scrub jungle type. From the succeeding Middle Palaeolithic stage, even the forest ecosystems of hilly zones began to be occupied. This was probably facilitated by the preparation of smaller tools permitting mobility and preparation of artefact types like points which could be used for hunting purposes. In the basin areas, a seasonal dispersal of hominin groups took place—clustering of hunting groups along streams with water-pools in their beds in dry season and dispersal all over the basins in the wet season. Murty also pointed out that in the early stages subsistence was essentially based on wild plants and that use of wild animals for food purposes became more common in the later stages. Thirdly, the occurrence of Neolithic pottery in the Mesolithic levels at Muchchatla Chintamanu Gavi and certain sculptural representations in stone belonging to the historical period show clearly that the absorption of elements of hunting-gathering way of life into the agricultural way of life and later into the Hindu fold had its beginnings in the terminal phase of the Stone Age itself.

In the Kaladgi basin of north Karnataka covering the Malaprabha and Ghataprabha valleys, Pappu and Deo (1994) followed up the initial investigations carried out by Joshi (1955) and Pappu (1974) and undertook a detailed study of the Stone Age sites from settlement pattern perspective. This revealed that the Stone Age groups avoided the forested and high rainfall tracts close to the Western Ghats and instead concentrated themselves on riverbanks and in the foothill zone of hills in the middle reaches of the rivers. The more recent excavation at Lakhmapur gave evidence of a transition from a late Acheulian stage to the Middle Palaeolithic (Petraglia, Schuldenrein and Korisettar 2003).

My own study of the Acheulian sites of the Hunsgi and Baichbal valleys in the Bhima basin of north Karnataka falls in this category. This work too involved three decades of field studies including excavation of three sites. The settlement system approach developed by Binford was adopted as an explicit research perspective in this study (Paddayya 1982, 2002). The two valleys, enclosed by shale-limestone tablelands or Archaean formations, are an erosional basin and cover an area of 500 km^2. Over 200 Acheulian sites were found in this basin. These mostly belong to the primary type and occur on the valley floor and in the foothill zone. Limestone was the principal raw material; and fossil fauna (wild cattle, horse, elephant, deer species, etc.) was also found in small quantities at some of the sites. Two major concentrations, each made up of 15 to 20 sites, and located at a stretch of 3 to 4 km., were found in the area—one along the Hunsgi stream in the Hunsgi Valley and the second along the Fatehpur nullah in the Baichbal Valley. The remaining sites were found scattered all across the valley floor. My ethnographic studies in the area spread over different seasons of the year showed that economically backward people still depend on large-scale exploitation of wild foods. These include 55 types of plant foods (fruits, seeds, gums, leafy greens, etc.) and 30 types of wild animal foods.

Pooling together these archaeological and ethnographic data, I proposed a model of the Acheulian settlement system of the Hunsgi and Baichbal valleys (Paddayya 1982: 61-95). This settlement system hinged on two principal seasonal resource management strategies: a) dry season aggregation of the Acheulian groups (as indicated by the cluster of archaeological sites) near perennial water-pools, as provided by spring flows in the Hunsgi nullah of the Hunsgi valley and at Mudnur in the Baichbal valley and reliance on large game hunging; and b) wet season dispersal of the groups all over the valley floor and emphasis on the exploitation of small fauna and plant foods.

My subsequent work in the two valleys was aimed at a more comprehensive understanding of the sites from the point of view of formation processes, leading to the recognition of functional variability among the sites in terms of hominin behaviour—manufacturing sites, occupation sites, food-processing sites, etc. (Paddayya and Petraglia 1995). This work also led to the discovery and excavation of the Isampur site, which is one of the best preserved and largest Acheulian manufacturing-cum-occupation sites in the Old World. The site covers an area of three-quarters of a hectare and the cultural horizon, associated with a weathered silicified limestone bed, underlay 1 to 2 m. thick silt deposit that had been quarried away by the Irrigation Department in 1985. Our excavations, covering an area of 159 m^2, exposed actual chipping areas and yielded over 20,000 artefacts in various stages of manufacture. Isampur gave fresh insights into the reduction processes employed for making various artefact types. The occurrence of animal fossils along with stone artefacts shows that the site was also an occupation site. It was a localized hub for manufacturing and occupation activities, from which the hominins radiated on to the uplands and the valley floor itself as part of their daily foraging activities (Paddayya, Jhaldiyal and Petraglia 2000, 2006). Samples of enamel extracted from bovid teeth found in excavation have been dated by ESR (electron spin resonance) method to 1.2 million years (Paddayya *et al.* 2002). My prolonged studies also made it possible to identify a three-phase evolution within the Acheulian culture of the Hunsgi and Baichbal valleys (Paddayya 2008b).

The above-mentioned prolonged projects undertaken by Misra, Murty and me, employing some of the New Archaeology's research strategies, in turn influenced several doctoral-level studies concerning specific regions in peninsular India. All these studies, aimed at the reconstruction of Palaeolithic and Mesolithic settlement and subsistence patterns, are based on intensive field studies of archaeological sites as well as ethnographic analogies drawn from the study of local hunting-gathering communities. Three of these dissertations deal, respectively, with the Late Upper Palaeolithic/Mesolithic sites of Koraput, Keonjhar and Phulbani districts of Orissa—all three areas receiving 75 to 100 cm of rainfall annually and covered with deciduous vegetation (Nanda 1985; Ota 1986; Mohanty 1993). It is but natural that adaptation to this ecological setting also required, in addition to light-duty blade tools of siliceous stones, a set of heavy-duty tools such as chopping tools, thick knives and scrapers on basic rocks like dolerite for wood-working purposes. Ethnographic analogies drawn from the study of simple societies such as the Gadabas, Juangs and Khonds gave useful clues for reconstructing the Stone Age settlement and subsistence strategies. D.R. Raju (1988) undertook intensive field studies and brought to light a large number of Stone Age sites (late Acheulian to Mesolithic in age) in the Gunjana Valley of Cuddapah district in Andhra Pradesh. He also made use of the ethnographic data concerning the wild plant and animal foods being used by the local Yanadi community for reconstructing the Stone Age settlement and subsistence patterns. Mention must also be made of Zarine Cooper's work on the Mesolithic sites around Chitrakot Falls on the river Mahanadi in central India (Cooper 1997a). She plotted extensive

Mesolithic scatters and documented the hunting and fishing activities of the local hunter-gatherer group called the Kurkus belonging to the Maria Gond tribe. She also carried out an excellent study of the hunting groups of the Andaman Islands and adopted the settlement system perspective for this purpose (Cooper 1992, 1997b).

Commencing with her doctoral research in the Kortallayar valley of northern Tamil Nadu in the 1990s, Shanti Pappu has since extended her Palaeolithic site survey to cover a larger area of 8000 km^2 (Pappu 2001; Pappu *et al.* 2011b). In addition to traditional methods of exploration and excavation, she made use of satellite remote sensing and GIS for understanding the geomorphic processes that operated on the ancient ferricrete landscape and the sedimentary and depositional contexts of Lower, Middlc and Upper Palaeolithic sites. Reference has already been made to the dating of the Acheulian levels from Attirampakkam excavation to 1.5 million years by direct 26 Al/Obl dating of buried stone artefacts. Also noteworthy is V. Selvakumar's study of the Mesolithic sites of the Gundar basin in Madurai district of Tamil Nadu from settlement system perspective (Selvakumar 1996).

The area, broadly called the northern Vindhyas and covering the Sidhi district and adjacent areas of Madhya Pradesh and Mirzapur district of Uttar Pradesh, has made known one of the richest concentrations of Stone Age sites in the country. Over the last half-century, the University of Allahabad, at times in collaboration with American and other foreign institutions, discovered a vast number of sites ranging in age from the Lower Palaeolithic to the Mesolithic (Sharma and Clark 1983). Also, excavations were conducted at some of these sites. These sites include both primary occurrences and secondary localities associated with fluviatile sediments. These occur either on the lower slopes of the Kaimur range of Vindhyan sedimentary rocks or on the sedimentary terraces and rocky ridges along the rivers Son and Belan and their tributaries. The published literature does not allow us as yet to make any elaborate inferences about the Stone Age settlement systems of northern Vindhyas but a significant finding concerning prehistoric ritual behaviour merits attention. This comes from the late Upper Palaeolithic site of Baghor I on the Son. Here, as part of an extensive occupation floor, a small triangular-shaped stone block with bright-coloured natural laminations was found. Based upon practices still current among local simple groups like the Kols, it has been suggested that the stone block was worshipped as a manifestation of Mother Goddess (Kenoyer *et al.* 1983). Damdama, Sarai Nahar Rai and Mahadaha were excavated and identified as semi-sedentary Mesolithic encampments located around horseshoe-shaped lakes in the Ganga Valley. These sites exposed rich stone tool assemblages, bone artefacts, floor levels with hearths, animal remains and remains of wild plant foods of various types besides human burials (Pal 2009). The late G.R. Sharma made the interesting observation that these sites represent summer encampments and that the human groups shifted to the Mirzapur hills further south across the Ganga River during the rainy season (Sharma 1973).

Further east, in the Paisra Valley of Munger district in Bihar, Pant and Jayaswal (1991) excavated primary context Acheulian levels yielding rich stone tool assemblages and structural features in the form of low stone walls and post-hole alignments: they visualized the prehistoric habitat in terms of a habitation zone and a zone meant for exploiting natural sources.

Protohistoric Studies

In protohisotric archaeology, there are some good case studies in which the New Archaeology's perspectives were employed for studying the early agro-pastoral cultures. In northern Deccan, H.D. Sankalia, M.N. Deshpande and others initiated the identification of a Chalcolithic phase in the 1950s and sites like Nevasa and Daimabad gave good evidence of both the sub-phases and their cultural components. But it was the decade-long (1972–82) horizontal excavations at Inamgaon initiated by Sankalia which exposed a full-fledged agro-pastoral settlement (houses, burials, belief system, technology, plant and animal remains) and made it possible to reconstruct the people's lifeways. This work was elevated to a qualitatively higher level with M.K. Dhavalikar's efforts to introduce the New Archaeology's major tenet of cultures as adaptational mechanisms (Dhavalikar 1988). He examined the origins and development of the Chalcolithic phase against the background of Holocene climatic history. His main proposition is that this phase started and flourished in the first half of the 2nd millennium BC due to a wet climatic phase conducive to agriculture, but by 700 BC the culture assumed a pastoral character specializing in sheep-goat husbandry due to a drastic fall in rainfall. Dhavalikar also made comments about aspects like demography, craft specialization, trade networks and ritual practices. Sheena Panja (1996) and Naik Mishra (1997) continued these studies and discovered several smaller settlements in the area as part of their regional approach to archaeological record. Also, Panja's ethnographic work on the Dhanagar pastoral community helped define various kinds of sites (permanent and temporary habitation sites, pastoral camps, etc.). All these studies made it possible to reconstruct the Chalcolithic phase in the

Deccan from settlement system perspective. Shinde's (1998) regional survey in the Khandesh area of upper Deccan led to the identification of Savalda, Late Harappan, Malwa and Jorwe cultural phases. Interpreting these sites from the point of view of settlement patterns, he pointed out that the Savalda and Late Harappan sites occur on the Tapi River itself, probably indicating a fair degree of dependence on agriculture. As against this, the Jorwe culture sites occur along the tributary streams; people relied more on sheep/goat pastoralism for which they exploited the pasture grounds of upper reaches of these feeder streams.

Another noteworthy study along these lines is that of Makkhan Lal (1984), which concerns the protohistoric sites of Kanpur district forming part of the upper portion of the Ganga-Yamuna Doab. Here the sequence comprises Late Harappan, OCP, Black and Red Ware, and Painted Grey Ware cultures. This study has shown how initially the feeder streams and eventually the Ganga and Yamuna themselves were occupied by the human groups. Also there was a perceptible increase in the density and sizes of settlements. In the Harappan studies proper, Singh and his team carried out a truly intensive survey of the hinterland of Rakhigarhi in Haryana, leading to the discovery of over 120 additional sites (Singh *et al.* 2010). This survey has many implications for understanding the rise and decline of Harappan urbanism in the region.

The work on the ashmounds of southern Deccan constitutes another noteworthy example of the beneficial effects of the use of developed theoretical perspectives. While ashmounds are known for the last two hundred years, the credit goes to Raymond Allchin for identifying this group of Neolithic sites as a problematic issue, for tackling which he adopted research strategies which already anticipated processual and post-processual schools. Adopting a regional approach, he explored all important ashmounds and this survey led him to propose the view that these were Neolithic cattle-pens. As Allchin himself clarified (1963: ix), his studies involved hypothesis raising and testing. He undertook excavation at Utnur and succeeded in obtaining structural and other forms of evidence relating to cattle-penning. He also interpreted that cow-dung burnings were part of a Neolithic ash-fire cult meant for promoting cattle fertility. His monograph *Neolithic Cattle-Keepers of South India: A Study of the Deccan Ashmounds* (1963) is a landmark publication in post-Independence archaeology and represents an excellent example of the complementary use of traditional archaeology and aspects of what we now call the New Archaeology and ideational archaeology.

I followed up this work on ashmounds in the 1990s. My own regional surveys and excavations at Budihal showed that the ashmounds were much more than cattle-pens (Paddayya 1993). Rather, they were full-fledged Neolithic pastoral settlements, with evidence of cattle-penning and cow-dung disposal, human occupation, burials and even an animal butchering floor as at Budihal (Paddayya 2002).

Megalithic monuments in India date to the Iron Age and occur in great numbers as five or six major types. Much of the work done on this topic is typological and classificatory. We have only a limited number of studies which deal with the landscape contexts and settlement and subsistence patterns of the Iron Age communities (Moorti 1994; Rajan 1994; Mohanty and Selvakumar 2002; Brubaker 2002). These studies were first initiated by S.B. Deo (1985) in the Vidarbha region.

HISTORICAL PERIOD

I would like to cite some examples of such studies in historical archaeology. George Erdosy (1988) took up a detailed field survey of the early historical sites of Allahabad district (ancient Vatsa Mahajanapada) and this enabled him to reconstruct the evolution of settlement patterns from the NBP phase to the Gupta period. Another interesting example concerns the famous complex of Buddhist monuments at Sanchi in central India. The discovery of this site took place nearly two hundred years ago. Since then much has been written about the art and architecture of the main stupa and other monuments on the hill. Also, the short one-line epigraphs on the stupa pillars gave James Prinsep the much-needed initial clues for the decipherment of Brahmi script. But the area around the site went practically untouched by archaeologists. This gap has now been filled up by Julia Shaw's detailed and prolonged investigations of the surrounding landscape. These brought to light excellent evidence of settlements and extensive irrigation works (Shaw 2000; Shaw and Sutcliffe 2001, 2003). It is this flourishing economic organization at the regional level which supported the large religious establishment. Lahiri (2011) undertook a similar landscape study with reference to the well-known site of Junagadh in Saurashtra. Such landscape studies are worth repeating at other major historical sites in the country. A fine example from Sri Lanka is provided by the settlement pattern studies of early and late historical sites of the Sigiriya-Dambulla region (Bandaranayake *et al.* 1990).

Another example of such studies concerns the famous medieval capital city of Vijayanagara in south India. Here also, all previous studies were confined to the imposing secular and religious monuments within the metropolis itself. To remedy the situation, as part of a comprehensive project, Sinopoli (2007) and her team took up intensive survey of the area around it within a radius of 10 to 15 km. This hinterland survey brought to light over 400 small and large sites representing both agricultural and industrial production processes. Other medieval sites in India still await planning of such settlement pattern studies.

INTERPRETIVE APPROACHES

Let us now turn to cases involving the application of soft perspectives forming part of post-processual archaeology. Rising above the long-held view which equated prehistoric research with stone tool descriptions and their functions, it is now being realized that the investigation of processes of raw material procurement and tool manufacture and use could give us valuable information about the cognitive abilities of Stone Age communities (Paddayya 2011a: 58-59). Also, attention has already been drawn to the ritual behaviour implied in the shrine-like structural feature and the small, triangular stone block with coloured laminations found in association with it at Baghor I on the Son River.

The archaeological record of the early agro-pastoral communities of the country offers tremendous scope for the use of ideational perspectives. Workers have already commented on several aspects of this archaeological record, e.g. female terracotta figurines of the Zhob Valley as manifestions of Mother Goddess; the bull figurines of Kayatha culture as fertility symbols; and the proto-Ganesh and Mother Goddess figurines found at Inamgaon (Sankalia 1977b; Dhavalikar 1988). The engraved design of a stag placed between two hunters (all with exaggerated genitals) and with two circles drawn above it (rising and setting sun?), as shown on a stone slab from Burzahom, has been interpreted in terms of phallicism or fertility cult (Pande 1971). Dhavalikar

(2009) interpreted the painted peacock designs on Cemetery H pottery at Harappa as signifying the concept of rebirth.

As pointed out earlier, Allchin's work on ashmounds, completed much before the rise of New Archaeology and later developments, made use of both adaptational and ideational perspectives. In particular, his interpretation of cow-dung accumulations and their burnings as forming part of a Neolithic fire-cult for promoting fertility of cattle, constitutes a good example of interpretive archaeology. While commending this work, I further proposed that these ashmounds, particularly the larger ones, served as monuments and promoted group identity. These were the spots where periodic regional congregations of the Neolithic groups probably took place, which promoted many socio-economic and ritual transactions (Paddayya 2005). Boivin (2004) put forward cosmological interpretations about the locational settings of some of the ashmounds. In her view, the locations of Kudatini and Toranagallu ashmounds in Bellary district were influenced by consideration of significant views, intersite visibility, cardinal directions and local solar events.

Coming to the Iron Age, reference has already been made to studies dealing with the locational settings and distribution pattern of sites containing megalithic monuments. The locational settings of the monuments of the upper Palar basin have been interpreted in terms of social stratification (Darsana 1998). Here the dolmens occur on hilltops and occupy a prominent position in the local landscape setting; these probably belong to a rich and socially dominant group within the community. The stone circles, on the other hand, are restricted to the foothill region and almost merge with the landscape, carrying little or no visibility value. These probably belong to the lower classes of the community. Interestingly, the megalithic monuments have also attracted the attention of astronomers and some interesting correlations have been put forward between placements of monuments or stone blocks within these and astronomical events like solstices (Kameswara Rao 2005). Pushpa Tiwari (2002) emphasized the need for taking up symbolic studies of rock art in India.

Symbolic perspectives have been used in medieval archaeology as well. The prolonged and multinational project at Vijayanagara involved detailed mapping of all kinds of features and structures, and their identification with the help of literary and epigraphical sources. The overall interpretation that was arrived at is that the Vijayanagara city was much more than the seat from which royal power was played out and much more than the nodal point of the interplay of socio-economic and political forces. It was simultaneously a symbolic expression of the celebrated epic city of Ayodhya. The layout of the royal residence, temples and other structural features, the circumambulatory depiction of movement around the royal residence, symbolizing *pradakshina* in a temple, and the mythological associations were all designed to evoke reference to the legendary capital of Ayodhya and the epic-hero Rama. In other words, the layout embodies the very principles that imbue royal actions with meaning and power. Indeed, the Vijayanagara city was the meeting ground of the king and the god. "King and God were the focus of the city: they paid homage to each other, and by radiating their energies outward they gave form, harmony, and plenty to the empire" (Fritz 1986: 53).

Finally, reference needs to be made to Daniel Miller's ethnographic study of the pottery of Dangwara village in Malwa region. This study is an attempt at introducing cognitive archaeology into the subcontinent (Miller 1985). Miller regards the traditional accounts of material culture variability in terms of technological and functional aspects as flawed, because they cannot explain the 'specificity' of variability. He rather treats artefacts as an aspect of the organization principles of human categorization processes and asserts that artefactual categories encode transactions involved in the production and reproduction of social life. Bringing these ideas to bear on Dangwara pottery, Miller detects in it much 'logic' for understanding distinctions of caste, family size and wealth. He further says that archaeologists could also adopt this approach, because the three aspects of rim shape, painted decoration and vessel morphology used by him in the Dangwara study also characterize pottery of the protohistoric and historical periods.

USE OF INDIGENOUS THEORETICAL PERSPECTIVES

While the foregoing examples no doubt illustrate the influences derived from processual and ideational archaeologies that came up in the Anglo-American world in the second half of the 20th century, it is important to realize that some of the basic tenets underlining these two streams of thought were already being put to use independently by workers in Indian archaeology before Independence. The following instances deserve attention.

The method of hypothesis, which was no doubt brought into prominence by the New Archaeology, actually has a much longer history cross-cutting all empirical sciences and played a crucial role in our understanding of both natural and humanly created worlds. Hypotheses are tentative and testable answers to questions that constantly arise about the nature of phenomena or their interconnections and origins. One can easily cite some examples of hypothesis use in Indian archaeology.

One of these concerns the decipherment of Brahmi script, which opened a rich source of information for the study of ancient Indian history. As is well known, James Prinsep gets a lion's share of the credit for its decipherment (Fig. 2.4). One of the crucial

Fig. 2.4 James Prinsep (1799–1840), Honorary Secretary of The Asiatic Society, Kolkata, who played a pivotal role in the decipherment of the ancient Indian scripts.

steps he took towards this end involved hypothesizing (Prinsep 1837). Struck by the analogy provided by the 18th century donative inscriptions which he had noticed in the Buddhist temples of Ava in Burma, Prinsep conjectured that the short one-line inscriptions found on the pillars at Sanchi stupa too recorded gifts or donations. More importantly, struck by the fact that the last three letters or alphabets of these pillar epigraphs were just the same, he hypothesized that these respectively stood for *sa, dâ* and *nam*—the Indo-Aryan word meaning "Of so and so gift" (Fig. 2.4a). Prinsep summed up the excitement that followed upon this breakthrough in these words:

> Since 1834 also my acquaintance with ancient alphabets had become so familiar that most of the remaining letters in the present examples could be named at once on reinspection. In the course of a few minutes I thus became possessed of the whole alphabet, which I tested by applying it to the inscription on the Delhi column... (Prinsep 1837: 461).

An equally enlightening example belonging to the mid-20th century is provided by the work on the Neolithic ashmounds of southern Deccan (Fig. 2.5). As we have noted earlier, these sites are known for the last two hundred years and various mythological, industrial and funerary interpretations were put

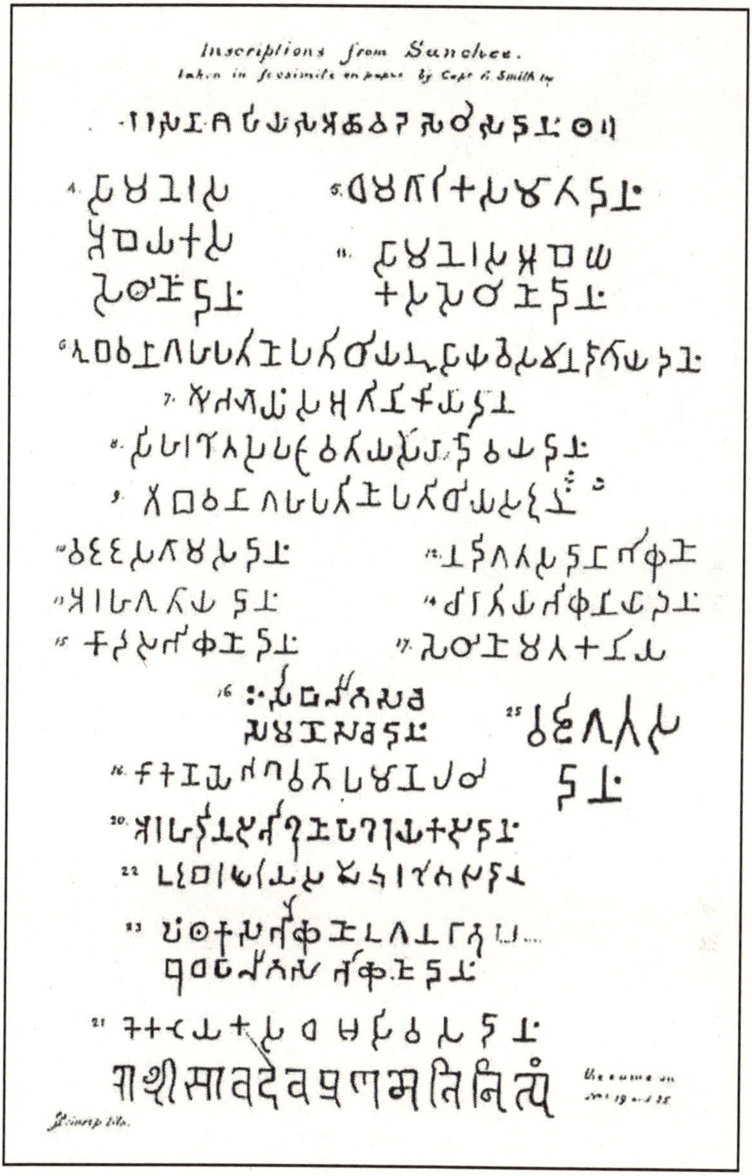

Fig. 2.4a James Prinsep's arrangement of one-line Brahmi inscriptions found on the pillars of Sanchi stupa, most of which end in the two letters—*da* and *nam*. After Prinsep 1837, Plate XXVII. Courtesy: The Asiatic Society, Kolkata.

Fig. 2.5 Frank Raymond Allchin (1923–2010) of Cambridge University —an outstanding spokesman of South Asian archaeology in the western world.

forward about their age and origin. Following Foote's inferences about the cow-dung origin of the deposits and based upon his own observations about the close spatial relationship between habitation and ashmound areas at Piklihal, Allchin made the initial inference about their cattle-pen origin. His subsequent field studies at other sites led him to develop this inference into a full-fledged hypothesis. For testing it, he took up a detailed excavation at Utnur. The confirmatory evidence from this excavation as well as ethnographic evidence he had obtained about place-names, present-day pastoral practices and pastoral elements in folk religion went into the preparation of his famous monograph *Neolithic Cattle-Keepers of South India* (1963). Allchin's work on ashmounds is an exemplification of the method of hypothesis advocated since long by the British empiricist philosophy of science and it also anticipated some of the cardinal propositions of both the New Archaeology and post-processual archaeology.

This brings us to the amazing realization that some aspects of interpretive archaeology, which lay emphasis on treatment of archaeological record as a text and as a repository of human motivations, feelings and emotions, were already foreshadowed in the Indian writings on texts, art and architecture. The tradition of interpretation, as applied to texts, is very old and is known as *tika* (elucidation) and *bhasya* (commentary) (Kapoor 1991). The hermeneutical tradition, which Julian Thomas and other archaeologists are employing in the study of the British Neolithic phase, has been used in India for reading the meanings of ancient texts ranging from the Vedic literature to the writings of medieval saints (Sundara Rajan 1991; Arapura 1986). For example, employing this perspective in his work on the writings of the saints of Maharashtra, Lele (1987) concluded that the writings of Sant Dnyaneshwar and Tukaram not only present a critique of the contemporary social order but at the same time offer an all-embracing blueprint for changing it (Sardar 1969). Archaeologists could employ it for studying the mute archaeological record.

Fig. 2.6 Ernest Binfield Havell (1861–1934), Principal of the Calcutta School of Art.

Reconstruction of the symbolic dimensions and contextual analysis of art objects and features in India for reaching their underlying meanings much predates the rise of symbolic archaeology in the West. This trend was pioneered by E.B. Havell, who came to India at the end of the 19th century as the principal of the Madras College of Art and later became the Principal of the Calcutta School of Art (Fig. 2.6). To Havell, understanding Indian art and its qualities meant understanding its sources of inspiration, its ideals and its symbolism. Contrary to the prevailing Eurocentric views, he emphasized that Indian art must be understood in terms of Indian thought. His stout defense of the Indian art in a public lecture he gave at the Royal Society of Art in London in 1910 brought a strong rebuttal from Sir George Birdwood. Ridiculing the Dhyanibuddha image and its symbolism, a photograph of which was put up by Havell as part of his lecture presentation, Birdwood blurted out:

> This senseless similitude in its immemorial fixed pose, is nothing more than an uninspired brazen image, vacuously squinting down its nose to its thumbs, knees and toes. A boiled suet pudding would serve equally well as a symbol of passionless purity and serenity of soul (as quoted by Keay 2001: 160).

Fig. 2.7 Ananda Kentish Coomaraswamy (1887–1947), the famed doyen of South Asian art historical studies.

Far from fading out, the trend set in motion by Havell was not only continued but further elaborated by Ananda Coomaraswamy (Fig. 2.7). This fresh orientation is reflected in Coomaraswamy's various writings from the 1920s through 1940s. His vast background knowledge of ancient Indian history, culture, religion and philosophy enabled him to formulate an interpretive trend which, while not denying the importance of "more mechanical tasks of description", ascribes symbolic meanings to art and architectural forms. He summarily rejected the view that symbolic meanings are 'read into' facts which originally had no meanings but only a physical efficiency (Guha-Thakurta 1992: Chapter 2). One or two examples will serve to illustrate the argument.

Emphasizing the role of empathy and contextual analysis for appreciating the symbolism of Buddha image, Coomaraswamy (1986: 147-48) wrote:

> In order to understand the nature of the Buddha image and its meaning for a Buddhist, we must, to begin with, reconstruct its environment. We must forget we are looking at 'art' in a museum and see the image in its place in a Buddhist church or as part of a sculptured rock wall and, having seen it, receive it as an image of what we are ourselves potentially. Remember that we are pilgrims coming from some great distance to see God, that what we see will depend upon ourselves. We are to see, not the likeness made by hands, but its transcendental archetype, we are to take part in a communion... The image is one of Awakened: and for our understanding, who are still asleep. The objective methods of 'science' will not suffice, there can be no understanding without assimilation; to understand is to have been born again.

Clearly, these are theoretical formulations which are valid for reading the meanings of many components of archaeological record.

Coming to the Hindu temple, Coomaraswamy viewed it not merely as a building giving shelter to the image; it is cosmos itself, the House of God and His body, representing in its parts the drama of disintegration and reintegration, which is the essential theme of Indian myth of creation and its ritual enactment in the sacrifice (Coomaraswamy 1938). This theme was subsequently developed further by Stella Kramrisch (1946) who treated the temple as the *Purusha* (a metaphorical representation of the creative force in the cosmos). In a similar vein Deshpande (1995) interpreted the famous rock-cut Kailash temple at Ellora as a symbolic expression of Advaita philosophy, which is premised upon the unity of all existence.

A fourth example from the study of Indian art involves the symbolism of Nataraja image. Havell had already drawn attention to the fact that the strong, muscular postures of Nataraja conceal the divine ecstasy of creation. Coomaraswamy elaborated upon this theme in his famous essay entitled "The Dance of Shiva". He attached threefold significance to the Nataraja image:

> ...First, it is the image of his Rhythmic Play as the source of all Movement within the Cosmos, which is represented by the Arch; Secondly, the purpose of his Dance is to release the countless souls of men from the Snare of Illusion; Thirdly, the place of the Dance, Chidambaram, the Centre of the Universe, is within the Heart.

Continuing his interpretation, Coomaraswamy further writes:

> In the night of Brahma, Nature is inert, and cannot dance till Siva wills it: He rises from His rapture and dancing sends through inert matter pulsing waves of awakening sound, and lo! matter also dances appearing as a glory round about Him. Dancing, He sustains its manifold phenomena. In the fullness of time, still dancing, he destroys all forms and names by fire and gives new rest. This is poetry, but none the less, science... (1985a: 65-66).

It is this notion of Shiva's dance, symbolizing matter in motion and cosmic cycles of creation and destruction, which has attracted the attention of physicists and astronomers. Fritjof Capra's best-selling book *The Tao of Physics* has made an elaborate reference to it (Capra 1991: 269-72). As he says,

> Modern (quantum) physics has thus revealed that every subatomic particle not only performs an energy dance, but also is an energy dance; a pulsating process of creation and destruction (Capra 1991: 271).

It was against this background of perfect correspondence between ancient Indian thought and findings of modern physics that a six-feet-tall metal image of Nataraja (presented by India) was installed on 16 June 2004 at the entrance of the famous European Centre for Nuclear Research (CERN) near Geneva (Fig. 2.8).

Fig. 2.8 Nataraja image installed in 2004 at the European Centre for Nuclear Research (CERN), Geneva.

There is one more instance of the germs of a dominant trend in Western social thought already finding expression in ancient Indian thought. This is the principle of binary opposites forming the core component of structuralism of Levi-Strauss. This principle underlies the Hindu conception of rhythmic character of the world-process. Coomaraswamy sums up the actual operation of this process in these eloquent words:

> This rhythm is determined by the great antithesis of Subject and Object, Self and not-Self, Will and Matter, Unity and Diversity, Love and Hate, and all other 'Pairs'. The interplay of these opposites constitutes the whole of sensational and registreable existence, the Eternal Becoming (*samâra)*, which is characterized by birth and death, evolution and involution, descent and ascent, *srishti* and *samhara.* Every individual life—mineral, vegetable, animal, human or personal god—has a beginning and end, and this creation and destruction, appearance and disappearance are of the essence of the world-process and equally originate in the past, the present and the future... (1985b: 10).

Instances like the ones cited above in fact call for a close examination of the possible relevance of ancient Indian epistemological traditions for studying the archaeological record.

In this regard I would like to reiterate what I have pointed out elsewhere (Paddayya 1995: 138-39). It is unfortunate that as yet nothing beyond an exploratory attempt has been made by archaeologists and historians (Dave 2009). Even a superficial analysis shows that the Indian conception of knowledge is a very elaborate one (e.g. Datta 1967). The Sanskrit word for cognition in general is *jnana* and valid cognition is called *prama.* The Hindu tradition recognizes a number of sources (*pramana*) of knowledge: perception, inference, authority, knowledge based on similarity (*upamana*), postulation (*arthapathi*), non-cognition, intuitive knowledge (*pratibha*) and unbroken tradition (*itiha*). Valid cognition is considered to be free from doubt (*samshaya*), indefiniteness (*anadhyavasaya*) and error (*bhrama*); it therefore reveals things as they are and furnishes the basis for successful activity.

In Hindu epistemology, the art of reasoning goes back to the Upanishads. The *Chandogya Upanishad* holds that reasoning with words (*vakovakya*) must be supported by experience and spiritual insights. In later texts like the *Manusmriti*, greater appreciation is expressed for this faculty of the human mind. It is however in the *Nyayasutra* of Gautama (suggested age varying from 4th century BC to 4th century AD) that we find its most elaborate expression. According to Gautama, doubt (*samshaya*) is the chief incentive to philosophical inquiry. He then goes on to prescribe an elaborate process for removing doubt. To put it in the words of Datta (1967: 132):

> One must consider carefully the pros and cons (*paksha-pratipaksha*) and ascertain the nature of things. For this purpose one is advised to take the help of all valid sources of knowledge, use (and avoid conflict with) previously established theories (*siddhanta*), use examples (*drishtanta*) which are acceptable to all, employ the five-step method of discovery and proof (*pancavayavanyaya*), use the indirect hypothetical or postulational methods of strengthening the conclusion (*tarka*), and also take care to avoid five kinds of material fallacies (*hetvabhasa*), three kinds of quibbles (*chala*), twenty-four kinds of false analogies (*jati*), and twenty-two kinds of self-stultifying steps, which would cause defeat in debates.

This elaborate method was not merely a matter of philosophical discourse but was meant to cover all domains of knowledge including the empirical sciences (see Seal 1915: 244-95). In fact, on reflection, one realizes that it is for all practical purposes identical with the scientific method as conceived in modern philosophy of science.

Another area of great potential use concerns ancient Indian notions of concepts, such as space, time, causality and explanation. Of special interest is the Buddhist theory of causation known as *paticca samuppada*, or dependent co-arising, which resembles general systems theory (see Jayatilake 1980; Macey 1992). In contrast to the linear notion of causation, the doctrine of *paticca samuppada* enunciated by the Buddha treats an event not as the result of one cause but as the concatenation of diverse, potentially causative factors into a unique relationship with one another. Thus, causality is seen as reciprocal and encompassing all phenomena—human and natural; it refers not merely to things and persons but to the processes connecting them together. Archaeologists in India need to seriously consider the application of this concept for investigating important topics like the origins and end of individual societal traditions as well as whole cultures including the Indus Civilization and empires of the historical period.

CONCLUSION

I would now like to conclude this chapter with one or two concluding remarks. On several occasions in Pune, Delhi and elsewhere, I have been asked by students and faculty alike to indicate the thought or school which is best suited to the needs of Indian archaeology—traditional culture history, the New (processual) Archaeology and post-processual (interpretive or ideational) archaeology. And add to these the Rightist, Leftist and such other schools (and their subdivisions) we have in India itself. Apparently, the whole scenario of theory use is confusing. It is similar to the mental predicament of the Kalamakas of Nalakagrama of northern India who complained to the visiting Buddha that they were puzzled by the proliferation of various teachings and were therefore unable to make a choice. The Buddha's reply was true to the spirit of a great teacher. Far from specifying any categorical criteria for accepting or rejecting a given teaching, he asks his interlocutors to use their own powers of observation and reason and then make a choice (Katz 1982: 205-06). It is no surprise then that the *Kalama Sutta*, which records this incident, is called the Buddha's charter of free enquiry (Soma Thera 1963). The Buddha's reply is relevant in our case too.

Despite occasional polemical stances put up by some of the workers, there are no inherent contradictions between these various schools of thought or 'isms' in archaeology. It is unthinkable that, without the background knowledge about it, the archaeological record of a given region could be approached from processual or interpretive points of view. The more mechanical tasks of establishing culture-sequences and description and classification of antiquarian remains could never be dispensed with. Likewise, even a staunch post-processualist like Hodder (1992: 169-80) had to admit that there are some positive methodological aspects of the New Archaeology which are vital to the discipline and that excesses have sometimes been committed in the name of interpretive archaeology. So it is not surprising that archaeologists have begun to show fresh interest in the New Archaeology (Bell 1994; Kuznar 1997).

In regions like India, it is very necessary that we keep in mind the complementary nature of various perspectives (Paddayya

2012b). Our archaeological record has an enormous time-depth spanning 1.5 million years. Secondly, even in the case of chronologically contemporaneous cultures, the record exhibits tremendous diversity across regions. Rather than blind allegiance to a particular research orientation, choice of any perspective should be guided by the level of prior knowledge that one has of the archaeological record of the area selected for study. There are many and vast areas in the country which are still archaeologically *terra incognita.* I estimate that these occupy more than 80% of the Indian landscape. Culture-history approach is the only meaningful way of initiating field research in these areas. In the case of areas already subjected to culture-history investigations and depending upon the nature of the archaeological record, processual and post-processual orientations could be employed for arriving at adaptational and ideational interpretations. I have cited earlier in this lecture some case studies in Indian prehistory which benefited from the employment of the New Archaeology propositions. These hold good even for the study of early agropastoral and later cultures, whose investigations also necessitate the use of some of the ideational perspectives (Paddayya 2011c: 13-14). Rather than being a linear process, in some cases the study may involve an interplay between various research orientations.

Finally, I hope that workers will rise above the level of treating theoretical debates as mere 'pleasant noises' and 'changes in trouser shapes' and, instead, treat these as essential to the growth of mature and scientific archaeology. There are some encouraging signs. At the Deccan College in Pune, the response of students to the incorporation of theory and method for teaching purposes has been quite positive. This in turn led to qualitative changes in the selection of topics for doctoral research. Themes such as human adaptations entailing the use of biological and earth sciences, settlement system studies, and investigation of formation process are now seen as meaningful research topics. This trend is catching up at other places too at both teaching and research levels.

REFERENCES

Agrawal, D.P. 1982. *Archaeology of India.* London: Curzon Press.

Agrawal, D.P. and J.S. Kharakwal. 2002. *South Asian Prehistory: A Multidisciplinary Study.* New Delhi: Aryan Books International.

——. 2003. *Bronze and Iron Ages in South Asia.* New Delhi: Aryan Books International.

Ajithprasad, P. 2007. Formation Processes of the Acheulian Sites of the Orsang Valley, Gujarat. In K. Paddayya, R. Jhaldiyal and S. Deo (eds.), *Formation Processes and Indian Archaeology,* pp. 79-91. Pune: Deccan College.

Allchin, B. (ed.). 1994. *Living Traditions.* New Delhi: Oxford-IBH.

Allchin, B. and F.R. Allchin. 1982. *The Rise of Civilization in India and Pakistan.* Cambridge: Cambridge University Press.

——. 1997. *Origins of a Civilization: Prehistory and Early Archaeology of South Asia.* New Delhi: Viking Penguin India.

Allchin, F.R. 1961. Ideas of History in Indian Historical Writing: A Preliminary Study. In C.H. Philips (ed.), *Historians of India, Pakistan and Ceylon*, pp. 241-59. London: Oxford University Press.

——. 1963. *Neolithic Cattle-Keepers of South India: A Study of the Deccan Ashmounds.* Cambridge: Cambridge University Press.

——. 1995. *The Archaeology of Early Historic South Asia: The Emergence of Cities and States.* Cambridge: Cambridge University Press.

Arapura, J.G. 1986. *Hermeneutical Essays on Vedantic Topics.* Delhi: Motilal Banarasidass.

Bandaranayake, M. Morgen and E. Seneviratne (eds.). 1990. *The Settlement Archaeology of the Sigiriya-Dambulla Region.* Colombo: Postgraduate Institute of Archaeology.

Bell, J. 1994. *Reconstructing Prehistory: Scientific Method in Archaeology.* Philadelphia: Temple University Press.

Binford, L.R. 1962. Archaeology as Anthropology. *American Antiquity* 28(2): 217-25.

——. 1964. A Consideration of Archaeological Research Design. *American Antiquity* 29(4): 425-41.

——. 1980. Willow Smoke and Dogs' Tails: Hunter-Gatherer Settlement Systems and Archaeological Site Formation. *American Antiquity* 45: 4-20.

Binford, Sally and L.R. Binford (eds.). 1968. *New Perspectives in Archaeology.* Chicago: Aldine.

Boivin, Nicole. 2004. Landscape and Cosmology in the South Indian Neolithic: New Perspectives on the Deccan Ashmounds. *Cambridge Archaeological Journal* 14: 235-57.

Boivin, Nicole and Dorian Q. Fuller. 2002. Looking for Post-processual Theory in South Asian Archaeology. In S. Settar and R. Korisettar (eds.), *Indian Archaeology in Retrospect* (Volume IV) – *Archaeology and Historiography (History, Theory and Method)*, pp. 191-215. New Delhi: ICHR and Manohar.

Brubaker, R. 2002. Aspects of Mortuary Variability in the South Indian Iron Age. *Bulletin of the Deccan College Research Institute* 60-61: 253-302.

Capra, Fritjof. 1991. *The Tao of Physics: An Exploration of the Parallels between Modern Physics and Eastern Mysticiem.* Third Edition. London: Flamingo. First Published in 1975.

Chakrabarti, D.K. 1989. *Theoretical Issues in Indian Archaeology.* New Delhi: Munshiram Manoharlal.

——. 2001. South Asia. In Tim Murray (ed.), *Encyclopaedia of Archaeology,* Volume III, pp. 1183-94. Santa Barbara, California: ABC-CLIO.

——. 2006. *The Oxford Companion to Indian Archaeology.* Delhi: Oxford University Press.

Chattopadhyaya, Indrani. 2000. Meaningful Action Considered as a Text. In S.C. Bhattacharya *et al.* (ed.), *Peeping through the Past*, pp. 131-39. Allahabad: University of Allahabad.

——. 2002. Habitus, Symbolic Archaeology and Interpretation of Archaeological "Text". In V.D. Misra and J.N. Pal (eds.), *Mesolithic India*, pp. 91-96. Allahabad: University of Allahabad.

Chattopadhyaya, Umesh. 2000. The Post-modern Denial of the Past: Challenges before Archaeology in Twenty-first Century. In S.C. Bhattacharya *et al.* (ed.), *Peeping Through the Past*, pp. 169-82. Allahabad: University of Allahabad.

Childe, V.G. 1956. *Society and Knowledge.* New York: Harper and Brothers.

Clarke, D.L. 1968. *Analytical Archaeology.* London: Methuen.

——. 1973. Archaeology: The Loss of Innocence. *Antiquity* 47: 6-18.

Clarkson, C. *et al.* 2009. The Oldest and Longest Enduring Microlithic Sequence in India: 35,000 Years of Modern Occupation and Change at the Jwalapuram Locality 9 Rock-shelter. *Antiquity* 83: 326-48.

Coomaraswamy, Ananda. 1938. Symbolism of the Dome. *Indian Historical Quarterly* 14: 1-56.

——. 1985a. The Dance of Shiva. In Ananda Coomaraswamy, *The Dance of Shiva—Essays on Indian Art and Culture,* pp. 56-66. New York: Dover Publications.

——. 1985b. What Has India Contributed to Human Welfare? In Ananda Coomaraswamy, *The Dance of Shiva—Essays on Indian Art and Culture,* pp. 1-17. Originally published in 1915. New York: Dover Publications.

——. 1986. The Nature of Buddhist Art. In R. Lipsey (ed.), *Coomaraswamy 1: Selected Papers (Traditional Art and Symbolism)*, pp. 147-78. Delhi: Oxford University Press. Originally published in 1938.

Cooper, Z. 1997a. *Prehistory of the Chitrakot Falls, Central India.* Pune: Ravish Publishers.

——. 1997b. The Salient Features of Site Location in the Andaman Islands, Indian Ocean. *Asian Perspectives* 36(2): 220-31.

——. 1992. The Relevance of the Forager/Collector Model in Island Communities in the Bay of Bengal. *Man and Environment* 17(2): 111-22.

Corvinus, G. 1981 and 1983. *A Survey of the Pravara River System in Western Maharashtra, India—Volume I: The Stratigraphy and Geomorphology of the Pravara River System; Volume II: The Excavations of the Acheulian Site of Chirki-on-Pravara, India.* Tübingen: Institut für Urgeschichte.

Daniel, Glyn E. 1967. *The Origins and Growth of Archaeology.* Harmondsworth: Pelican Books.

——. 1975. *150 Years of Archaeology.* London: Duckworth.

Darsana, S.B. 1998. Megaliths in the Upper Palar Basin, Tamil Nadu: A New Perspective. *Man and Environment* 23(2): 51-64.

Datta, D.M. 1967. Epistemological Methods in Indian Philosophy. In C.A. Moore (ed.), *Indian Mind: Essentials of Indian Philosophy and Culture,* pp. 118-35. Honolulu: University of Hawaii Press.

Dave, Hemant. 2009. *Scientific Method in Archaeology: An Indian Epistemological Perspective.*Unpublished Ph.D. Thesis. Pune: Deccan College.

Dennell, R.W. 2009. *The Palaeolithic Settlement of Asia.* Cambridge: Cambridge University Press.

Deo, S.B. 1985. The Megaliths: Their Culture, Ecology, Economy and Technology. In S.B. Deo and K. Paddayya (eds.), *Recent Advances in Indian Archaeology*, pp. 89-99. Pune: Deccan College.

Deshpande, M.N. 1992. Influence of the Philosophy of Sankaracharya on Hindu Temple Architecture and Symbolism. *Man and Environment* 28(1): 21-28.

Dhavalikar, M.K. 1984. Toward an Ecological Model for Chalcolithic Cultures of Central and Western India. *Journal of Anthropological Archaeology* 3: 133-58.

——. 1988. *The First Farmers of the Deccan.* Pune: Ravish Publishers.

——. 1997. *Indian Protohistory.* New Delhi: Books and Books.

——. 1999. *Historical Archaeology of India.* New Delhi: Books and Books.

——. 2009. Cemetery H Revisited: Probing the Harappan Mind. In K. Paddayya, P.P. Joglekar, K.K. Basa and R. Sawant (eds.), *Recent Research Trends in South Asian Archaeology,* pp. 183-89. Pune: Deccan College.

Erdosy, G. 1988. *Urbanization in Early Historic India.* Oxford: BAR International Series.

Fairservis, Jr. Walter A. 1971. *The Roots of Ancient India: The Archaeology of Early Indian Civilization.* New York: The Macmillan Company.

Fritz, J.M. 1986. Vijayanagara: Authority and Meaning of a South Indian Imperial Capital. *American Anthropologist* 88: 44-55.

Fuller, Dorian Q. and Nicole Boivin. 2002. Beyond Description and Diffusion: A History of Processuel Theory in the Archaeology of South Asia. In S. Settar and R. Korisettar (eds.), *Indian Archaeology in Retrospect: Archaeology and Historiography (History, Theory and Method),* Volume IV, pp. 159-90. Delhi: ICHR and Manohar.

Guha-Thakurta, T. 1992. *The Making of a New 'Indian' Art: Artists, Aesthetics and Nationalism in Bengal 1850-1920.* Cambridge: Cambridge University Press.

Hodder, Ian. 1992. *Theory and Practice in Archaeology.* London: Routledge.

Jacobson, J. 1975. Early Stone Age Habitation Sites in Eastern Malwa. *Proceedings of the American Philosophical Society* 119: 280-97.

Jayatileke, K.N. 1980. *Early Buddhist Theory of Knowledge.* Delhi: Motilal Banarasidass. First published in 1963.

Joshi, R.V. 1955. *Pleistocene Studies in the Malaprabha Basin, Karnataka.* Pune: Deccan College.

Kameswara Rao, N. 2005. Aspects of Prehistoric Astronomy in India. *Bulletin of the Astronomical Society of India* 33: 499-511.

Kapoor, Kapil. 1991. Some Reflections on the Interpretation of Texts in the Indian Tradition. In H.S. Gill (ed.), *Structure of Signification,* Volume 1, pp. 208-71. New Delhi: Wiley Eastern Ltd.

Katz, Nathan. 1963. *Buddhist Images of Perfection.* Delhi: Motilal Banarasidass.

Keay, John. 2001. *India Discovered: The Recovery of a Lost Civilization.* New Delhi: Harper Collins Publishers.

Kennedy, K.A.R. 2000. *God-Apes and Men: Palaeoanthropology of South Asia.* Ann Arbor: University of Michigan Press.

Kenoyer, J.M., J.D. Clark, J.N. Pal and G.R. Sharma. 1983. An Upper Palaeolithic Shrine in India? *Antiquity* 58: 88-94.

Kramrisch, Stella. 1975. The Temple as Purusha. In P. Chandra (ed.), *Studies in Indian Temple Architecture,* pp. 40-46. Delhi: American Institute of Indian Studies.

Kuhn, T.S. 1962. *The Structures of Scientific Revolutions.* Chicago: Chicago University Press.

Kuznar, L.A. 1997. *Reclaiming a Scientific Anthropology.* Walnut Creek (California): Altamira Press.

Lahiri, Nayanjot. 2006. Archaeological Theory: A Perspective from Outside the Western Academy. *Puratattva* 36: 1-11.

———. 2011. Revisiting the Cultural Landscape of Junagadh in the Time of the Mauryas. *Puratattva* 41: 115-30.

Lal, Makkhan. 1984. *Settlement History and the Rise of Civilization in the Ganga-Yamuna Doab from 1500 BC–300 AD.* Dehli: B.R. Publishing Corporation.

Lele, J. 1987. Jnaneshwar and Tukaram: An Exercise in Critical Hermeneutics. In M. Israel and N.K. Wagle (ed.), *Religion and Society in Maharashtra,* pp. 115-30. Toronto: Centre for South Asian Studies.

Macey, J. 1992. *Mutual Causality in Buddhism and General System Theory: The Dharma of Natural Systems.* Albany: State University of New York Press.

Malik, S.C. 1965. *Stone Age Cultures of the Bombay and Satara Districts.* Vadodara: M.S. University.

——. 1968. *Indian Civilization—The Formative Period: A Study of Archaeology as Anthropology.* Simla: Indian Institute of Advanced Study.

——. 1975. *Understanding Indian Civilization: A Framework of Enquiry.* Simla: Indian Institute of Advanced Study.

Mate, M.S. 2005. *Archaeology of Medieval India.* Delhi: B.R. Publishing Corporation.

Miller, Daniel. 1985. *Artefacts as Categories: A Study of Ceramic Variability in Central India.* Cambridge: Cambridge University Press.

Mishra, Sheila. 1995. Chronology of the Indian Stone Age: The Impact of Recent Absolute and Relative Dating Attempts. *Man and Environment* 20: 11-16.

Mishra, Sheila, N. Chauhan and A. Singhvi. 2009. Earliest Dated Microlithic Site of Mehtakheri, District West Nimar, Madhya Pradesh, India: Implications for the Archaeology of Modern human Dispersals. In M.K. Murari *et al.* (eds.), *Second Asia Pacific Conference on Luminescence and Electron Spin Resonance Dating* (Abstracts), 12-15 November 2009. Ahmedabad: Physical Research Laboratory.

Mishra S., S. Deo, R. Abbas, S. Naik, G. Shete, N. Agrawal and S.N. Rajaguru. 2009b. Excavations at the Early Acheulian Site of Morgaon, District Pune (2000-2007): A Report. In K. Paddayya, P.P. Joglekar, K.K. Basa and R. Sawant (eds.), *Recent Research Trends in South Asian Archaeology,* pp. 121-37. Pune: Deccan College.

Misra, V.D. and J.N. Pal (ed.). 1997. *Indian Prehistory: 1980.* Allahabad: University of Allahabad.

———. 2002. *Mesolithic India.* Allahabad: University of Allahabad.

Misra, V.N. 1973. Bagor—A Late Mesolithic Settlement in Northwest India. *World Archaeology* 5(1): 92-110.

———. 1978. The Acheulian Industry of Rock-shelter III F-23 at Bhimbetka, Central India—A Preliminary Study. *Australian Archaeology* 8: 63-106.

———. 1985. The Acheulian Succession at Bhimbetka, Central India. In V.N. Misra and P. Bellwood (eds.), *Recent Advances in Indo-Pacific Prehistory*, pp. 35-47. New Delhi: Oxford and IBH Publishing Co.

———. 1987a. Middle Pleistocene Adaptations in India. in O. Soffer (ed.), *Pleistocene Old World: Regional Perspectives,* pp. 99-114. New York: Plenum Press.

———. 1987b. Evolution of the Landscape and Human Adaptation in the Thar Desert. Presidential Address of Anthropology and Archaeology Section, 74th Session of Indian Science Congress, Bangalore.

———. 1989. Stone Age India: An Ecological Perspective. *Man and Environment* 14: 17-64.

———. 1990. The Van Vagris: 'Lost' Hunters of the Thar Desert, Rajasthan. *Man and Environment* 15(2): 89-108.

———. 1995. Evolution of Environment and Culture in the Rajasthan Desert during the Late Quaternary. In E. Johnson (ed.), *Ancient Peoples and Landscapes,* pp. 77-103. Lubbock, Texas: Texas Technical University Press.

———. 2002. Mesolithic Culture in India: Keynote. In V.D. Misra and J.N. Pal (eds.), *Mesolithic India,* pp. 1-66. Allahabad: University of Allahabad.

Mohanty, P.K. 1993. Mesolithic Hunter-Gatherers of Keonjhar District, Orissa. *Asian Perspectives* 85-104.

Mohanty, P. and J. Mishra. 2002. Fifty Years of Ethnoarchaeological Research in India: A Review. In S. Settar and R. Korisettar (eds.), *Indian Archaeology in Retrospect,* Volume III - *Archaeology and Interactive Disciplines,* pp. 169-207. New Delhi: ICHR and Manohar.

Mohanty, R.K. and V. Selvakumar. 2002. The Archaeology of the Megaliths in India. In S. Settar and R. Korisettar (eds.), *Indian Archaeology in Retrospect*, Volume I—*Prehistory*, pp. 313-51. New Delhi: ICHR and Manohar.

Moorti, U.S. 1994. *Megalithic Culture of South Asia: Socio-Economic Perspectives*. Varanasi: Ganga Kaveri Publishing House.

Murty, M.L.K. 1968. Blade and Burin Industries near Renigunta on the Southeast Coast of India. *Proceedings of the Prehistoric Society* 34: 83-101.

——. 1974. A Late Palaeolithic Cave Site in Southern India. *Proceedings of the American Philosophical Society* 118: 196-230.

——. 1979. Recent Research on the Upper Palaeolithic Phase in India. *Journal of Field Archaeology* 6(3): 301-20.

——. 1981. Hunter-gatherer Ecosystems and Archaeological Patterns of Subsistence Behaviour on the Southeast Coast of India: An Ethnographic Model. *World Archaeology* 12: 47-58.

——. 1985. Ethnoarchaeology of the Kurnool Cave Areas. *World Archaeology* 17: 192-205.

Nagar, Malti. 2008. *Hunter-Gatherers in North and Central India: An Ethnoarchaeological Study*. Oxford: BAR International.

Nagar, M. and V.N. Misra. 1993. The Pardhis: A Hunting-Gathering Community of Central and Western India. *Man and Environment* 18(1): 115-40.

Naik, S. and S. Mishra. 1997. Chalcolithic Phase in the Bhima Basin—A Review. *Man and Environment* 22(1): 44-58.

Nanda, S.C. 1985. The Microlithic Cultures of the Indravati Valley, District Koraput, Orissa. In V.N. Misra and P. Bellwood (eds.), *Recent Advances in Indo-Pacific Prehistory*, pp. 159-65. New Delhi: Oxford and IBH.

Ota, S.B. 1986. Mesolithic Culture of the Phulbani District (Orissa), with Special Reference to Heavy-Duty Implements. *Bulletin of the Deccan College Research Institute* 45: 47-56.

Paddayya, K. 1978a. Review of H.D. Sankalia's book *New Archaeology: Its Scope and Application to India. Indica* 15: 158-63.

———. 1978b. New Research Designs and Field Techniques in the Palaeolithic Archaeology of India. *World Archaeology* 10: 94-110.

———. 1979. Palaeoethnography *vis-à-vis* the Stone Age Cultures of India: Some Methodological Considerations. *Bulletin of the Deccan College Research Institute* 38: 63-90.

———. 1980. On the Threshold (A Review Article on the Recent Developments in Method and Theory in Archaeology). *Bulletin of the Deccan College Research Institute* 39: 117-34.

———. 1981. Piaget, Scientific Method and Archaeology. *Bulletin of the Deccan College Research Institute* 40: 235-54.

———. 1982a. Ecological Archaeology and the Ecology of Archaeology: The Archaeologist's Viewpoint. *Bulletin of the Deccan College Research Institute* 41: 130-50.

———. 1982b. *The Acheulian Culture of the Hunsgi Valley (Pennisular India): A Settlement System Perspective.* Pune: Deccan College.

———. 1983. Myths About the New Archaeology. *Saeculum* 34: 70-104.

———. 1984. India: Old Stone Age. In H. Mueller-Karpe (ed.), *Neue Forschungen zur Altsteinzeit,* pp. 345-503. Munich: C.H. Beck Verlag.

———. 1985. Theoretical Archaeology: A Review. In S.B. Deo and K. Paddayya (eds.), *Recent Advances in Indian Archaeology,* pp. 6-22. Pune: Deccan College.

———. 1986. The Epistemology of Archaeology: A Postscript to the New Archaeology. *Bulletin of the Deccan College Research Institute* 45: 89-115.

———. 1989. The Role of Hypothesis and Traditional Archaeology. *Bulletin of the Deccan College Research Institute* 47-48 (1988-89): 239-47.

———. 1990. *The New Archaeology and Aftermath: A View from Outside the Anglo-American World.* Pune: Ravish Publishers.

——. 1993. The Ashmounds of South India: Fresh Evidence and Possible Implications. *Bulletin of the Deccan College Research Institute* 51-52: 573.

——. 1995. Theoretical Perspectives in Indian Archaeology: A Historical Review. In Peter J. Ucko (ed.), *Theory in Archaeology: A World Perspectives*, pp. 110-49. London: Routledge.

——. 2001. The Acheulian Culture Project of the Hunsgi and Baichbal Valleys; Peninsular India. In L. Barham and K. Robson-Brown (eds.) *Human Roots: Africa and Asia in the Middle Pleistocene*, pp. 235-58. Bristol: Western Academic Press.

——. 2002a. A Review of Theoretical Perspectives in Indian Archaeology. In S. Settar and R. Korisettar (eds.), *Indian Archaeology in Retrospect*, Volume IV—*Archaeology and Historiography: History, Theory and Method*, pp. 117-57. New Delhi: ICHR and Manohar.

——. 2002b. The Problem of Ashmounds of Southern Deccan in the Light of Recent Research. In K. Paddayya (ed.), *Recent Studies in Indian Archaeology*, pp. 81-111. New Delhi: Munshiram Manoharlal.

——. 2005. Symbolic Approaches to the Study of Early Agro-Pastoral Communities of Lower Deccan. *Puratattva* 35: 1-6.

——. 2008a. South Asia: Palaeolithic Cultures. In Deborah M. Pearsall (ed.), *Encyclopedia of Archaeology*, Volume 1, pp. 768-91. Oxford: Elsevier and Academic Press.

——. 2008b. Evolution within the Acheulian: A Case Study from the Hunsgi and Baichbal Valleys, Karnataka. *Bulletin of the Deccan College Research Institute* 66-67 (2006-07): 95-111.

——. 2009. Contributions of Robert Bruce Foote to Indian Prehistory. In K. Paddayya, P.P. Joglekar, K.K. Basa and R. Sawant (eds.), *Recent Research Trends in South Asian Prehistory*, pp. 171-80. Pune: Deccan College.

——. 2011a. Stone Age Technology in India. *Ancient India* (New Series) 1: 9-68.

——. 2011b. The Place of the Past in the Indian Mind. *Journal of the Asiatic Society* 53: 1-18.

——. 2011c. Newer Perspectives in the Investigation of Early Agro-Pastoral Cultures of India. *Man and Environment* 36(2): 1-19.

——. 2012a. Lewis Binford and the Deccan College Connection. *Bulletin of the Deccan College Research Institute* 70-71 (2010-11): 157-64.

——. 2012b. Some Topical Issues in Contemporary Archaeology in India (Shri A. Ghosh Memorial Lecture). New Delhi: Archaeological Survey of India.

Paddayya, K. *et al.* 2002. Recent Findings on the Acheulian of the Hunsgi and Baichbal Valleys, Karnataka, with Special Reference to the Isampur Excavation and Its Dating. *Current Science* 83(5): 641-57.

Paddayya, K., R. Jhaldiyal and S.G. Deo (eds.). 2007. *Formation Processes and Indian Archaeology*. Pune: Deccan College.

Paddayya, K., R. Jhaldiyal and M.D. Petraglia. 2000. The Significance of the Acheulian Site of Isampur, Karnataka, in the Lower Palaeolithic of India. *Puratattva* 30: 1-24.

——. 2006. The Acheulian Quarry at Isampur, Lower Deccan. In Nama Goren-Inbar and Goren Sharon (eds.), *Axe Age: Acheulian Tool-Making from Quarry to Discard*, pp. 45-73. London: Equinox.

Paddayya, K. and M.D. Petraglia. 1995. Natural and Cultural Formation Processes of the Acheulian Sites of the Hunsgi and Baichbal Valleys, Karnataka. In S. Wadia, R. Korisettar and V.S. Kale (eds.), *Quaternary Environments and Geo-archaeology of India*, pp. 333-51. Bangalore: Geological Society of India.

Pal, J.N. 2009. Recent Researches in the Archaeology of the Ganga Plain and the Vindhyas. In K. Paddayya, P.P. Joglekar, K.K. Basa and R. Sawant (eds.), *Recent Research Trends in South Asian Archaeology*, pp. 165-79. Pune: Deccan College.

Pande, B.M. 1973. Neolithic Hunting Scene on a Stone-slab from Burzahom Kashmir. *Asian Perspectives* 14: 134-38.

Panja, S. 2002. The Third Space: The Creation of Archaeological Knowledge in Post-Independence India. *Studies in History* 18: 1-22.

Pappu, R.S. 1974. *Pleistocene Studies in the Upper Krishna Basin.* Pune: Deccan College.

——. 2001. *Acheulian Culture in Peninsular India: An Ecological Perspective.* New Delhi: P.K. Printworld.

Pappu, R.S. and S. Deo. 1994. *Man-Land Relationships during Palaeolithic Times in the Kaladgi Basin.* Pune: Deccan College.

Pappu, Shanti. 2001. *A Re-Examination of the Palaeolithic Archaeological Record of Northern Tamil Nadu, South India.* Oxford: BAR International Reports.

Pappu, S. *et al.* 2011a. Early Pleistocene Presence of Hominins in South India. *Science* 331 (March 2011): 1596-99.

Pappu, S., Kumar Akhilesh, Sudha Ravindranath and Uday Raj. 2011b. From Stone Tools to Satellites: Recent Research into the Prehistory of Tamil Nadu. *Ancient India* (New Series) 1: 87-100.

Petraglia, M.D., J. Schuldenrein and R. Korisettar. 2003. Landscapes, Activity, and the Aheulian to Middle Palaeolithic Transition in the Kaladgi Basin, India. *Eurasian Prehistory* 1(2): 3-24.

Petraglia, M.D. *et al.* 2007. Middle Palaeolithic Assemblages from the Indian Subcontinent Before and After the Toba Super-eruption. *Science* 317: 114-16.

Pratap, Ajay. 2009a. The Relevance of Processual *vs.* Post-processual Archaeology: A Debate for Theoretical Archaeology in India. *Puratattva* 39: 27-37.

——. 2009b. *Indigenous Archaeology in India: Prospects for an Archaeology of the Subaltern.* Oxford: Archaeopress. BAR International Series.

Prinsep, James. 1837. Note on the Facsimiles of Inscriptions from Sanchi near Bhilsa, Taken for the Society by Captain Ed. Smith, Engineers; and on the Drawings of the Buddhist Monument, Presented by Captain W. Murray, at the meeting of the 7th June. *Journal of the Asiatic Society of Bengal,* Volume VI: 451-77.

Rajan, K. 2000. *South Indian Memorial Stones.* Thanjavur: Manoo Pathippakam.

Raju, D.R. 1988. *Stone Age Hunter-Gatherers: An Ethnoarchaeology of Cuddapah Region, South-east India.* Pune: Ravish Publishers.

Russell, Bertrand. 1976. *The Problems of Philosophy.* Oxford: Oxford University Press. Published in 1912.

Sali, S.A. 1989. *The Upper Palaeolithic and Mesolithic Cultures of Maharashtra.* Pune: Deccan College.

Sankalia, H.D. 1962. *Prehistory and Protohistory in India and Pakistan.*Mumbai: University of Bombay. Revised edition published as *Prehistory and Protohistory of India and Pakistan* in 1974. Pune: Deccan College.

——. 1977a. *Prehistory of India.* Delhi: Munshiram Manoharlal.

——. 1977b. *New Archaeology: Its Scope and Application to India.* Lucknow: Ethnographic and Folk Culture Society.

——. 1979. *Indian Archaeology Today.* Delhi: Ajanta Publications.

Sardar, G.M. 1969. *The Saint-Poets of Maharashtra: Their Impact on Society* Mumbai: Orient Longman.

Seal, B. 1915. *The Positive Sciences of the Hindus.* London: Longmans, Green Co.

Sharma, G.R. 1973. Mesolithic Lake Cultures in the Ganga Valley. *Proceeding of the Prehistoric Society* 39: 129-46.

Sharma, G.R. *et al.* 1980. *Beginnings of Agriculture (Epi-Palaeolithic to Neolithic)– Excavations at Chopani-Mando, Mahadaha and Mahagara.* Allahabad: University of Allahabad.

Sharma, G.R. and J.G.D. Clark (eds.). 1983. *Paleoenvironments and Prehistory in the Middle Son Valley, Northern Madhya Pradesh.* Allahabad: University of Allahabad.

Shaw, Julia. 2000. Sanchi and Its Archaeological Landscape: Buddhist Monasteries, Settlements and Irrigation Works in Central India. *Antiquity* 74: 775-76.

Shaw, Julia and J.V. Sutcliffe. 2001. Ancient Irrigation Works in the Sanchi Area: An Archaeological and Hydrological Investigation. *South Asian Studies* 17: 55-75.

Shinde, V.S. 1998. *Early Settlements in the Tapi Basin.* New Delhi: Munshiram Manoharlal.

Shrimali, K.M. 2009. People's Archaeology and Archaeology for the People: Y.D. Sharma Memorial Lecture. *Puratattva* 39: 172-94.

Singh, Rameshwar. 1965. *Palaeolithic Industries of Northern Bundelkhand.* Unpublished Ph.D. thesis, University of Pune.

Singh, R.N. *et al.* 2010. Changing Patterns of Settlement in the Rise and Fall of Harappan Urbanization and Beyond: A Preliminary Report on the Rakhigarhi Hinterland Survey 2009. *Man and Environment* 35(1): 37-53.

Singh, Shivaji. 1985. *Models, Paradigms and the New Archaeology.* Varanasi: Banaras Hindu University.

Sinopoli, Carla M. 2007. Formation Processes and the Vijayanagara Metropolitan Survey. In K. Paddayya, R. Jhaldiyal and S. Deo (eds.), *Formation Processes and Indian Archaeology*, pp. 161-70. Pune: Deccan College.

Soma Thera (ed. and tr.). 1963. *Kalama Sutta: The Buddha's Charter of Free Inquiry.* Kandy: Buddhist Publication Society.

Subbarao, B. 1958. *The Personality of India.* 2nd Edition. Vadodara: M.S. University.

Sundara Rajan, R. 1991. *Studies in Phenomenology, Hermeneutics and Deconstruction.* New Delhi: Indian Council of Philosophical Research.

Taylor, W.W. 1948. *A Study of Archaeology. American Anthropologist* 50, Memoir No. 69. Washington, D.C.: American Anthropological Association.

Tewari, Pushpa. 2002. Aesthetics and Mesolithic Art and Artefacts: An Analysis of the Underlying Principles of Art in Mesolithic India. In V.D. Misra and J.N. Pal (eds.), *Mesolithic India*, pp. 428-446. Allahabad: University of Allahabad.

Thapar, B.K. 1985. *Recent Archaeological Discoveries in India.* Tokyo: UNESCO and Centre for East Asian Studies.

Thomas, J. 1991. *Rethinking the Neolithic.* Cambridge: Cambridge University Press.

——. 1996. *Time, Culture and Eternity: An Interpretive Archaeology.* London: Routledge.

Trigger, B. 1985. *Archaeology as Historical Science.* Varanasi: Banaras Hindu University.

——. 1989. *A History of Archaeological Thought.* Cambridge: Cambridge University Press.

Wheeler, R.E.M. 1949. Archaeological Fieldwork in India: Planning Ahead. *Ancient India* 5: 4-11.

——. 1960. *Early India and Pakistan.* London: Thames and Hudson.

CHAPTER III

Don't We Need More "Falls Through the Roof"?

"I fell into Indology, as it were, through the roof." This was the expression used by the late D.D. Kosambi to describe the non-professional route, which he had adopted for initiating his own study of ancient Indian past (Kosambi 1972). I suppose readers could easily guess that my answer to the interrogative contained in the title of this chapter would be a resounding 'Yes'. I believe that unlike back-door entries, which are rarely free from negative colourings, roof-entries afford a bird's-eye view of the entire scenario. Kosambi's work is an awe-inspiring example of the benefits of roof-entry approach (Fig. 3.1). I for one firmly believe that academic custodians of the past stand to benefit immensely by lending their ears for a while to what others have to say about the past: its sources, contents and uses which it is put to. In this chapter I would like to illustrate my observations by way of drawing attention to the writings of some prominent non-specialists. Let us start with Kosambi himself.

D.D. KOSAMBI'S INSIGHTS INTO PREHISTORY

Like his father Dharmanand Kosambi, Damodar Kosambi occupies a unique place in modern Indological studies. Formally

Fig. 3.1 D.D. Kosambi (1907–1966), the mathematician who "fell into Indology through the roof".

belonging to the discipline of mathematics, he entered the domain of the study of ancient India out of genuine interest in the past and, as was expected of a person with a scientific bent of mind and a deep urge to understand the origins and development of ancient Indian society from the point of view of cultural processes and patterns, brought a new whip of air to the whole pursuit. It is appropriate that, as a mark of respect to his memory, some special volumes have been published and also some seminars have been held in different parts of the country during the last 35 years (e.g. Sharma 1974; Habib 1974; a special issue of *Economic and Political Weekly* 2008; Jha 2011). Also, a volume containing his collected essays has been published (Chattopadhyaya 2002).

Adopting an interdisciplinary methodological strategy and also the Marxian perspective of history as consisting of successive stages of development in the means as well as relations of production, Kosambi put forward his own views about the development of the formative phase of Indian history. It is true that objections have been raised to some of his views, e.g. linking the end of the Harappan culture with the entry of Aryans, the importance of iron technology in the genesis of early historical urbanism, and the rise of feudalism (e.g. Dhavalikar 2008). These objections themselves are far from flawless and still there is a general consensus among historians that Kosambi shook the foundations of historical research in India by his interrogative bent of mind and forced workers to rethink about many long-held interpretations and the methodologies used for arriving at these.

As a specialist in prehistory, I am glad to draw the attention of readers to the fact that Kosambi, in a 27-page long chapter entitled 'Primitive Life and Prehistory' forming part of his famous book *The Culture and Civilization of Ancient India in Historical Outline* (1965), made some very insightful observations about the Stone Age communities of tropical regions like India. These deserve close attention on the part of prehistorians (Paddayya 2011a: 11):

a) Ice Age was not as harsh and extensive as in Europe, so that food-gathering was a much easier task and included a wide range of edible items.
b) Culture refers to the essential ways of life of people.
c) Food supplies are an essential basis of human cultures and their procurement is dependent on the tools and techniques devised for this purpose.
d) Advances in procurement strategies lead to both alterations in the relations of production and population rise.
e) Chronologically speaking, cultural development is far from uniform but varies from region to region.
f) 'Living prehistory' or ethnography is an important methodological strategy of Stone Age research.

Nearly half a century thenceforth, where do we stand in Indian prehistory? Stone Age studies in India have a history of 150 years. For well over a century these were obsessed with stone tool collections and classification, so much so that Sir Mortimer Wheeler (1960: 34, 63) was provoked to dub Indian prehistory as a matter of "Stones" and "More Stones". But one is happy to note that, due to the influence of processual trends initiated by the New Archaeology and, to some extent, thanks to the proddings of historians like Kosambi, some important changes have been initiated during the last three decades or so (Paddayya 1978, 2008). Irfan Habib's book *Prehistory* (2001) is a small but helpful introduction to the study of Stone Ages as a cultural science. The following aspects merit attention.

The workers realized the need to rise above the level of type-fossil approach to Stone Age cultures and reorient their studies in terms of palaeoethnography (Paddayya 1979) or what Kosambi called "essential ways of life of the people." In lieu of search for secondary context sites such as those associated with river gravels and silts, emphasis now began to be laid on the investigation of *in situ* or primary sites and their excavation in a systematic way in order to understand the true character of Stone Age technology (raw material selection, flaking processes and typological composition). The settlement system perspective developed by the New Archaeology also brought home the need for adopting a regional perspective in field studies in order to understand the differences in the nature and sizes of sites and also their locational contexts. Another important methodological strategy concerned the use of ethnographical analogies drawn from the study of extant hunting-gatherer societies, more particularly their exploitation of wild animal and plant foods on a seasonal basis. In the case of the Acheulian culture of Hunsgi and Baichbal Valleys of north Karnataka, two principal resource management strategies were recognized: a) dry season aggregation of hunter-gatherer groups near spring pools and reliance on large game hunting and b) wet season dispersal and exploitation of plant foods and small animals (Paddayya 1982).

Prehistorians in India also started realizing the truth value of Kosambi's (1965: 34) observation that, lacking the rigour of true Ice Ages in tropical lands, the Stone Age groups in India would have depended less on animal foods and more on plant foods such as fruits, nuts, seeds, berries, bulbs, leafy vegetables, honey and mushrooms. Ethnographic studies in the Bhima, Kurnool and Cuddapah basins have shown that simple communities, such as the Chenchus, Yanadis and Uppars, still make use of a wide variety of plant foods (Murty 1981, 1985; Paddayya 1982; Raju 1988). Plant remains are difficult to recover from the Stone Age archaeological record but some important clues have been obtained in recent times. Archaeobotanical remains of wild bread fruit (*Artocarpus nobilis*), a wild nut (*Canarium zeylanicum*) and two species of wild banana have been reported from the Mesolithic levels (dated to 8,000 to 10,000 years BP) at the sites of Belilena Kitulgala and Batadombalena in Sri Lanka (Kajale 1989). Kajale (1996) has also identified seeds of wild plants assignable to Chenopodiaceae, Polygonaceae and other families from the Mesolithic site of Damdama in the Ganga basin. Indirect clues about exploitation of wild plant foods have also been noted at the Acheulian site of Yediyapur in Baichbal Valley of north Karnataka (Paddayya 2010). The excavated lithic assemblage from this site includes a class of artefacts called crushers. These are flat-sided, oval-shaped implements, which show marks of scarring along the blunt periphery, probably resulting from crushing and pounding of soft materials like plant foods.

Equally insightful is Kosambi's observation that Stone Age cultural development was regionally variable and far from uniform across the whole country. Field research undertaken during the last three to four decades fully supports this inference. Relative dating facilitated by stratigraphical data and chronometric dates obtained by absolute dating methods have revealed wide chronological variability in regional cultural developments. Regions like northeastern India are good examples of secondary prehistory and witnessed the initiation of cultural developments at a much later stage in comparison with peninsular India. Even within the latter region, there are wide temporal disparities from area to area. For example, the Lower Palaeolithic stage in Rajasthan is dated to 0.4 million years BP, while in the Bhima and Kortallayar basins of peninsular India it stretches back to 1.2/1.5 million years BP. Likewise, the Middle Palaeolithic stage in Rajasthan has an antiquity of 0.15 million years, while in the Ganga-Yamuna zone it is assigned to 45,000 years BP. The beginning of microlithic tradition stretches back to 35,000 to 40,000 years BP in the Narmada and Kurnool areas, while in most other areas in the country the Mesolithic phase belongs to the early Holocene.

No less conspicuous is the regional variability in terms of cultural contents within each one of the major stages of prehistoric sequence. Far from treating these individual cultural stages any longer as pan-Indian entities, prehistorians have now realized that there is a need for studying these major phases as comprising a series of regional adaptive systems with organizational identities of their own, arising from geographical differences in terrain morphology, availability of raw materials, plant and animal foods, and water sources.

Kosambi was a Marxist to the extent, and only to the extent, that he considered food supplies and means of their procurement (means and relations of production, to use Marxian phraseology) as a dominant factor in the functioning and development of human societies. To be sure, in archaeology, there were voices earlier emphasizing economic aspects of past societies. *Prehistoric Europe: The Economic Basis* by Grahame Clark (1952) is a well-known publication in European archaeology. In the New Archaeology of Binford, ecological and subsistence factors once again occupy a primary position in hunter-gatherer societies. But what is important to note is that Kosambi made his observations totally unaware of the views of archaeologists. The available studies permit us to infer that improvements in raw material use and technological processes did lead to significant developments in the Stone Age societies of India. The increasing use of siliceous materials for tool-making from the Middle Palaeolithic phase onwards and the predominant use of flake- and blade-tools which are smaller than bifacial tools surely enabled people to occupy newer regions and exploit additional resources.

Also, these technological improvements led to more intensive exploitation of some of the areas and this in turn promoted demographic rise. This has been proved correct in the case of intensively surveyed areas. My own work in the Hunsgi and Baichbal valleys of north Karnataka brought to light about two hundred Acheulian (Lower Palaeolithic) sites in an area of 500 km^2. When we come to the Mesolithic stage, the number of sites increases to such an extent that it is difficult to recognize where one site ends and another starts. My estimate is that population density rose from one person per 2 km^2 in the Acheulian stage to about five persons per square kilometer in the Mesolithic period.

Another major innovative contribution made by Kosambi to Indological studies concerns his emphasis on multidisciplinary approach, particularly the use of combined methods of anthropology, archaeology and linguistics. The various essays in his book *Myth and Reality* (1962) are an excellent example of the relevance of ethnographic approach or what he called living prehistory in historical and archaeological studies. This was at a time when Indian archaeologists were preoccupied with recovery of antiquarian remains from the field and hardly realized the relevance of the present for approaching the past. It is only since the 1970s that ethnoarchaeology has emerged as a regular branch of Indian archaeology (Sengupta *et al.* 2006).

PSYCHOANALYSTS AND PHILOSOPHERS

There are other classes of non-professional writers who also took deep interest in the study of the country's early past and even felt inspired to write about it or interpret it. They too came out with some interesting interpretations and views of their own. Let us examine some of these writings.

Sudhir Kakar is a well-known psychoanalyst and is rated by some among 25 major thinkers of the world. His two books, *The Inner World: Psychoanalytical Study of Childhood and Society in India* (2008) and *The Indians: Portrait of a People* (2007)—the latter jointly with his wife Katharina Kakar—are an important attempt to understand the nature of the Indian psyche. These works arose from long experiences with their patients, their own reading of the ancient Indian texts and anthropological understanding of the Indian way of life. The Kakars consider the following four as the principal components or building blocks of the Indian identity: a) an ideology of family and other crucial human relationships derived from the institution of joint family; b) social relations which are essentially governed by caste considerations; c) an understanding of the human body and its various processes, basically derived from Ayurveda; and d) a cultural imagination replete with many shared myths and legends drawn particularly from the two great epics *Ramayana* and *Mahabharata* and envisaging a romantic vision of human life and context-dependent way of thinking. Sudhir Kakar has reiterated these aspects of the Indianness in a more recent publication entitled *India Analysed* (2009: 67).

The Kakars hold the cultural ensemble as a critical component of the spirit of India. What is this ensemble made up of? To put the matter in their own words:

> ...Here we are not concerned so much with philosophical doctrines that are relevant only for religious and intellectual elites but with the beliefs and attitudes—many of them not conscious—of a vast number of Indians that are reflected in their lives, their songs and their stories. These beliefs are disseminated through myths and legends, proverbs and metaphors, enacted in religious rituals, conveyed through tales told to children... The world-view that we are talking about, then, is absorbed from early on in life and not through the head but the heart (Kakar and Kakar 2007: 181).

Employing Freudian psychoanalytical perspectives, Sudhir Kakar attempts to reconstruct the psycho-social background of the Indianness and observes that the individual's superego is built on the model of superego of parents. Elaborating this point, Kakar (2008: 15) writes:

> An exploration of the psychological terrain of the Indian world must begin with the cluster of ideas, historically derived, selected and refined, through which Hindu culture has traditionally structured the beliefs and behaviours of its members. At the heart of this cluster of governing ideas is a coherent, consistent world image in which the goal of human existence, the way to reach this goal, the errors to be avoided and the obstacles to be expected along the way are all dramatically conveyed. I am not talking here of Hindu philosophy in the sense of abstract intellectualized concepts accessible only to an elite priesthood of interpreters, but of

> prescriptive configuration of ideal purposes, values and beliefs which percolate into the everyday life of ordinary people and give it form and meaning.

That a sense of the past forms an inalienable component of the Indian psyche has been emphasized in an equally forceful way by another social analyst and thinker. In a thought-provoking essay entitled "History's Forgotten Doubles", Ashis Nandy (2002) stoutly defends the Indians' construction of their past and its use. He says that this construction represents an alternative *to* (sic) history; it is history's doubles. He elaborates his point of view in these words:

> However odd this might sound to contemporary historians, millions of people still live outside history. They *do* (sic) have theories of the past; they do believe that the past is important and shapes the present and the future but they also recognize, confront and live with a past different from the one constructed by historians and historical consciousness. They even have a different way of arriving at the past (Nandy 2002: 83).

Nandy further says that in this construction, experiences of the past are organized mostly through myths, which are essentially morality tales. Secondly, unlike the historians who are bound by norms of fact-finding and objectivity, the people's construction of the past adopts elastic guidelines while scanning the sources so as to render historical consciousness less impersonal and more humane. Nandy cites the psychoanalyst Girindra Sekhar Bose's study of the Puranas and epics, undertaken in the early part of the last century, as an example of this form of history-writing.

A similar conception of the past has been voiced by the philosopher D.P. Chattopadhyaya. In his book *The Ways of*

Understanding the Past (2001), he argues that, while Homer's works the *Iliad* and the *Odyssey* may have disappeared from contemporary Greek life, the epics *Mahabharata* and *Ramayana* and their numerous regional editions are still a living force in the Indian way of life and in fact constitute a form of history called *itihasa.* V.S. Pathak (1966), Romila Thapar (1984, 1991, 1992, 2013) and Arvind Sharma (2003) have commented on the historical context of *Itihasa* tradition. The academic or scientific conception of history is guided by spatio-temporal and causal parameters. In contrast to this conception,

> ...In *Itihasa* legendary tradition is creatively blended with symbolic myths and tales with a view to conveying some spiritual and social uses to the people at large ... In these works, aesthetic emotion, poetry, fiction and romance are imaginatively mingled with philosophy, ethics and social and political ideas. Though the epics are dominated by the narrative consideration of the main stories, the underlying ethico-religious (*dharma*) tone is unmistakable (Chattopadhyaya 2001: 55).

JURISTS

Then there is the case of jurists who have produced their own commentaries on aspects of Indian history, culture and thought. In western India we have some famous examples. Justice M.G. Ranade not only made the Bombay Presidency government open the Peshwa Daftar records in Pune to scholarly research but he himself wrote his famous book *Rise of the Maratha Power* in 1900 (Fig. 3.2). In this book, Ranade proposed the view that the establishment of the Maratha empire was much more than a political event associated with a single personality. Rather, it represented an upheaval of the whole population, strongly bound

Fig. 3.2 Mahadev Govind Ranade (1842–1901), an eminent jurist and early nationalist leader.

together by the affinities of language, race, religion and literature. He even suggested that this was the first attempt at nation-making. In his own words:

> ...It was not a mere Political Revolution that stirred Maharashtra towards the close of the sixteenth and the commencement of the seventeenth centuries. The political revolution was preceded, and in fact to some extent caused, by a religious and social upheaval which moved the entire population... (Ranade 1961: 4).

Vasudeva Kirtikar (a Judge of the Bombay High Court) wrote an excellent commentary on the Upanishads entitled *Studies in Vedanta* (1924). It runs to about 200 pages and comprises ten papers that were previously published between 1904 and 1909 on various aspects of the Upanishads. Concluding his detailed review of this book, Gurudev R.D. Ranade (2001: 109) wrote:

> We can see from the above how very widely read Mr. Kirtikar was, what insights he had in Vedantism, how he could compare different points of view from Eastern and Western thought, what a lucid style he could write, what a life he held out to his own ideal and the ideal of those who were like him, and how finally for all these reasons the work under review is a work of exceedingly high value for the student of comparative thought...

Another well-known example is provided by Mahamahopadhyaya P.V. Kane who was first a schoolteacher, then a lawyer at the Bombay High Court and, finally, a Professor of Law (1917–23) at the Government Law College in Bombay. His five-volume monumental work on ancient Indian legal thought entitled *History of the Dharmasastras* was published between 1930 and 1962, and runs to 6,500 pages. As Radhakrishnan said in a Foreword to the last volume, Kane's work helps us "understand what is living and what is dead in the heritage which has come down to us." Many such examples can be cited from other parts of the country. One such example of recent times is provided by Justice Markandey Katzu's essay on Indian culture (Katzu 2012). It is an excellent piece of writing arising from a speech delivered by him to non-resident Indians in California in 2011 and captures all important aspects of ancient Indian culture and thought including the linguistic contributions of Panini.

OTHER WRITERS

We then have a general class of thinkers and writers represented by persons such as Raja Ram Mohan Roy, Aurobindo, Vivekananda and Rabindranath Tagore who came out with their own assessments of ancient Indian thought. Writing about Tagore's visualization of India's past, Bhattacharya (2011a: 67-84; see also 2011b: Chapter 6) states that Tagore recognized that India, unlike the Western civilization which decimated the local cultures in different parts of the world, developed a syncretic civilization. Tagore further argued that, unlike the state-centred European civilization, the Indian civilization maintained its continuity through the society and culture of the people (Fig. 3.3). In a memorable passage, Tagore wrote in 1902:

> ...the aim of Bharatavarsha has always been to establish unity amidst differences (or diversities), to bring to a convergence of different paths, and to internalize within her soul the unity of the severalty, that is to say, to comprehend the inner union between externally perceptible differences without eliminating the uniqueness of each element.... Bharatvarsha has endeavoured to tie up diversities in a relationship... (as quoted by Bhattacharya 2011a: 70).

Fig. 3.3 Gurudev Rabindranath Tagore (1861–1941), the first Nobel Laureate from Asia.

What has the Nobel Laureate Amartya Sen to say about the past? He has set forth his views in an essay entitled *On Interpreting India's Past*, which arose from a lecture he had delivered at The Asiatic Society in Kolkata in March 1995 (Sen 1996a; see also 2001). Sen readily grants that the past consisting of shared memories and recollections is an important cementing medium in the formation of a society's or group's self-identity. While noting the overarching unity of Indian culture, as was highlighted by Nehru and other nationalist leaders, Sen emphasizes that our understanding of contemporary India should be more fully cognizant of the divisions and fragments that make up the nation. His advocacy of strong socio-cultural and political pluralism within the country finds best expression in a review article on

Satyajit Ray's films and writings, entitled, "Taking Pride in a Pluralistic Society" (Sen 1996b). Sen identifies three underlining themes in Ray's work: a) individuality of each local or regional culture; b) the heterogeneous character of culture at local, regional and national levels; and c) need for intercultural communication. Sen prescribes a two-element methodology for facilitating intercommunication, viz. a) positional objectivity which provides for multiple ways of looking at a given situation or event, leading to interpersonal understanding; and b) subjecting the latter to practical reason for assessing their implications while contemplating action in the present.

Sen sums up his views about the place of the past in the present in these eloquent words:

> The interpretation of India's past cannot but be sensitive to the concerns of today. Our identities cannot be defined independently of our traditions in the past, but this does not indicate a linear sequence whereby we interpret our past first, and then arrive at our identity, equipped to face contemporary issues. On the contrary, our reading of the past and understanding of the present are interdependent, and the selectional criteria that are Entral to interpreting the past have to take note of the relevance of the different concerns in the contemporary world. While we cannot live without the past, we cannot live within it either (Sen 1996a: 38; see also 2001).

In his later publications, Sen, as part of his larger concept of welfare economics, proposed a new definition of development as freedom (Sen 1999). Sen's view of development is an agent-centered process in which individuals, far from being treated as passive beneficiaries, are viewed as agents effectively contributing to the formulation of public policy. Their participatory capabilities are enhanced by drawing upon social values and mores, for which the past is a rich source in the Indian context.

VIEWS OF WRITERS FROM OUTSIDE INDIA

Fig. 3.4 Bruce Rich, a noted American attorney and environmentalist.

Interestingly, there are also cases of non-specialist writers from outside the country evincing deep interest in India's early past. Bruce Rich is a Senior Attorney and head of an environmental organization in the U.S. (Fig. 3.4). In 2008, he published a fairly large book entitled *To Uphold the World: The Relevance of Ashoka and Kautilya for the 21st Century.* As indicated by the subtitle itself, Rich puts forward a fervent plea that the two great personalities of India antedating the Christian era by a few hundred years have true relevance in the modern world—the *Arthasastra* prescriptions of Kautilya for coming to grips with the manifold material transactions of the globalized world and the tenets of Asoka's *Dhamma* policy for wading through the moral dilemmas of modern societies. It is important to realize that Rich's book is not a hurried attempt making use of a few selected source materials of secondary origin but actually arose from a deep study of the primary sources including the *Arthasastra* and Asoka's edicts themselves. Emphasizing their contemporary relevance, Rich writes:

> ...What I had hoped to do is to examine them (the principles and precepts enshrined in the writings of Ashoka

> and Kautilya) as archetypes, metaphors and sources of inspiration for thinking about the perennial conundrums of politics, economics and ethics, which today are played out on a global scale as never before... my hope has been to offer a personal contribution to showing the relevance of a part of ancient Indian thought and history to the challenges of the 21st century (Rich 2008: xv).

Like Gandhi, Ashoka appears to have captured in recent years the imagination of the public in the West. Wijze Keyuing, a schoolteacher in the Netherlands, wrote a book on Ashoka in Dutch between 1941 and 1947. It has now been translated into English and published in 2011 under the title *Ashoka the Great* (Keyuing 2011). This book rather belongs to the genre of historical novels and highlights the ideals which the emperor stood for. A little later I will make a reference to another recent book on Ashoka.

NATIONALIST LEADERS

Bipin Chandra Pal, one of the early nationalist leaders from Bengal, wrote a series of four letters to one of his friends in the U.S.; these were published in 1911 under the title *The Soul of India.* Pal once again emphasized the pluralistic character of Indian civilization. Neither the Hindu society nor the Hindu religion, in Pal's view, is a single unit; both are federations of many units. "The freedom and integrity of the parts inside the unity of the whole, is the very soul and essence of the federal idea" (Pal 2000: xiii). In his well-known book *The Arctic Home in the Vedas*, Bal Gangadhar Tilak argued in favour of the polar origins of the Aryans (Tilak 1903). His commentary on the *Bhagavadgita* laid emphasis on the path of action; he adopted it too as a method in his nationalist struggle (Tilak 1935).

Nehru holds a prominent place among the nationalist leaders of India. Although he obtained his Tripos in natural sciences from Cambridge University, his interest in history basically developed out of his desire to educate his school-going daughter Indira about man and world history. In the summer of 1928, he wrote a series of 30 letters to the ten-year-old Indira attending school in Mussorie (Nehru 1993). Written in simple and lucid language, these letters touch upon topics ranging from the origin of the earth to the place of the epics *Ramayana* and *Mahabharata* in the Indian way of life. Many years later, from prison, he wrote to the grown-up girl Indira another series of letters later published as *Glimpses of World History* (Nehru 1962). This is a fascinating account of the entire story of man from prehistoric to modern times through ancient and medieval periods. His vision of history was universalistic in scope; it was influenced by humanistic philosophy (Gokhale 1978). This finds expression in the famous passage on 'To what I am heir?' in *The Discovery of India,* in which he declares:

> To all that humanity has achieved during tens of thousands of years, to all that it has thought and felt and suffered and taken pleasure in, to its cries of triumph, to that astonishing adventure of man which began so long ago and continues and beckons us. To all this and more, in common with all men (1960: 9).

While in the two publications comprising his letters citied above Nehru was playing the role of a history teacher by proxy, he was performing a 'teach-yourself-history' job in his work *The Discovery of India* (1960). Written within the four walls of Ahmadnagar prison in the thick of freedom struggle, Nehru wanted to understand his country and its people by providing himself with an additional window by way of delving into their past. It was far from his desire to add another volume to the shelves of books on Indian history. So there is not much force in the statement that *The Discovery of India* is "a great jumble of a book" and an example of "woolly writing" (Gopal 1976: 298).

Nehru gave eloquent expression to his views about the ultimate relevance or purpose of history in the opening chapter of *The Discovery of India*. He writes:

> I came late to history and, even then, not through the usual road of learning a mass of facts and dates and drawing conclusions and infereness from them, unrelated to my life's course… The roots of the present lay in the past and so I made voyages of discovery into the past, ever seeking a clue in it, if any such existed, to the understanding of the present (Nehru 1960: 9).

Emphasizing further that the country's past loses its importance *sans* its bearing on the present, Nehru states further:

> …The past oppresses or fills me sometimes with its warmth when it touches on the present, and becomes as it were an aspect of that living present. If it does not do so, then it is cold, barren, lifeless, uninteresting… (1960: 22).

Irfan Habib (2011) has correctly pointed out that Nehru's writings reflect his wide range of readings, concern for accuracy and breath of perspective. Further, Nehru wanted his understanding of the past not only to brighten his grasp of the present but also provide clues for preparing an action plan to build a secular and pluralistic India at a future date. Josh (2012), for example, describes at length the role played by Nehru in the selection of Ashokan lion-capital and *chakra* from Sarnath as emblems for the new nation.

Mahatma Gandhi is another nationalist leader who made elaborate comments on the ancient Indian past

Fig. 3.5 Mohandas Karamchand Gandhi (1869–1948), Father of the Nation.

(Fig. 3.5). Barring his *Hind Swaraj* first published in 1909 (Gandhi 2006), these observations never took the form of a book or longish essays. Rather, these are in the form of answers to questions or form part of writings on other topics (e.g. Gandhi 1955). Like Nehru, Gandhi had little use for conventional history in the form of chronicles of kings and wars. He called it the vertical coordinate (Gokhale 1972; see also Iyer 1973). He did recognize the occurrence of change in man's life from the stage of hunter-gatherer to that of the agriculturist and then to the stage of civilized life. But to him this change is not so much a matter of progress in material well-being. Rather, it represents man's perennial or ceaseless quest to be at peace with himself and with society of which he is a part. True to his well-known spiritual way of looking at things around him, Gandhi believed that both the individual person and the society are confronted with a conflict between divine and devilish forces and that man's progress lies in conquering the evil "till he has become like unto God". This rise of man towards God is not to be calibrated in terms of decades or centuries but as cycles of ages forming part of the cosmic process.

To Gandhi the horizontal coordinate of history is formed by myths and legends, allegories and parables, which in the case of

India are derived from ancient texts such as the two epics and Puranas. He was a votary of *Sanatana Dharma* or Indian identity. He viewed the following as its main components: a) universe as one vast *yajna*; b) permeation of cosmic spirit in all creation; c) indivisibility of man; d) viewing all human actions as grateful offerings at the cosmic altar (Parekh 1995: 85-109). Like Tagore, Gandhi too was struck by the assimilative spirit of Indian civilization (Bhattacharya 2011a: Chapter 2).

Gandhi's aversion to industrial civilization and its dehumanizing trends are well known. Instead, he put enormous faith and respect in the peasant, who in fact becomes the hero of his historical thinking. Based upon his readings of the works of Ruskin and Tolstoy and of course his extensive tours across the Indian landscape, Gandhi formed the strong belief that the peasant's work is life-creating, while industrial civilization is life-destroying. It is therefore not surprising that he envisions a Golden Age characterized by a peasant-centred society of numerous village republics. This is his concept of *Rama Rajya* in which history and mythology lose their distinctions and man discovers his own humanity, which is but a mirror of the Supreme.

WRITINGS ON HISTORY OF ARCHAEOLOGY

Finally, we come to an aspect which is even closer to our hearts as archaeologists. This is about the history of archaeology. Indological studies have a history of two centuries and a quarter. Alexander Cunningham (1871: 1-43) made the first survey of the development of antiquarian studies. Over the last half century, a large number of publications (books and papers) dealing with this long story of investigations have appeared. These range from

Sourindranath Roy's book *The Story of Indian Archaeology from 1784 to 1947* published in 1961 to H.P. Ray's publication *Colonial Archaeology in South Asia: The Legacy of Sir Mortimer Wheeler* which came out in 2008. Written as they are by professionals, these publications are rightly preoccupied with major events, facts and dates. As with professional accounts of history and archaeology, these writings do not appear to have generated much interest among educated laymen about the whole saga of archaeological discoveries.

Recent years have witnessed a pleasant development, which seems to fill up this gap. Several publications by non-professional writers have appeared in print on this topic. These narratives are peppered with anecdotes of curiosity, romance and adventure with the Indian landscape (natural and cultural) and are well suited to take the saga of discovery of India's past to the doorsteps of the common people. John Keay's book *India Discovered: The Recovery of a Lost Civilization* (2001a) is one such example (Fig. 3.6). It seeks, and with remarkable success, "to convey something of the wonder of each new discovery and the excitement of each new deduction" (2001a: 14). Keay feelingly recounts the feats and efforts of a series of pioneer antiquarian workers ranging from Sir William Jones and James Prinsep to James Fergusson and E.B. Havell to

Fig. 3.6 John Keay (1941–), Scottish writer and historian.

surveyors and cartographers, such as Colin Mackenzie, William Lambton and George Everest.

Noteworthy too are Keay's two other books. These are *When Men and Mountains Meet: The Explorers of the Western Himalayas 1820-75* (2003), and *The Great Arc: The Dramatic Tale of How India was Mapped and Everest was Named* (2000a). The former book gives a truly absorbing account of how the Western Himalayas such as the Pir Panjals, Karakorams, Hindu Kush and Kun Lun were surveyed and mapped in the 19th century. Going beyond the academic orientations adopted by Phillimore (1945–54) and Edney (1997) while dealing with the history of cartography in India, in *The Great Arc* Keay recounts the trials and tribulations experienced by the staff of the Great Trignometrical Survey. He provides a truly fascinating account of how William Lambton and George Everest measured by means of the triangulation method the heights and coordinates of a whole series of locations along a 1600-mile long line stretching from Cape Comorin to the Himalayas. The Great Indian Arc, as this long and inch-perfect plotted line of locations has been called, served as the basis for other surveys in the country. It is no surprise then that it has been hailed as "one of the most stupendous works in the history of science".

Keay's other book, *The Honourable Company* (2001b), documents the history of the East India Company. In *India: A History* (2000b) he provides a rapid but well-grounded history of India from the Harappan times up to Independence and beyond. Keay has come out with another very interesting book entitled *To Cherish and Conserve* (Keay 2011). He has been commissioned by the National Culture Fund, New Delhi, to write this book as part of the celebrations marking the completion of 150 years of the Archaeological Survey of India. This is a short but very lucid account both of the background for the establishment of the Survey in 1861 and of the achievements made by it in various branches in the initial four decades. Keay has skilfully blended information about major advances and discoveries with details about policy decisions of the colonial government. The book will be widely welcomed by all who have an interest in knowing about the development of studies dealing with India's archaeological heritage including its conservation.

Charles Allen's *The Buddha and the Sahibs* (2002) is another eminently readable book and offers a fascinating account of the contributions made by the early colonial workers towards the recognition of Buddhism as a separate religion. He has documented in great detail the painstaking efforts made by Francis Buchanan, Coin Mackenzie, Alexander Cunningham and several others to probe the various kinds of archaeological vestiges scattered all over the landscape. Allen's other book *The Buddha and Dr. Führer* (2010) exposes the scandal involving Dr. Führer's faking of the relics of Buddha recovered from the stupa excavation at Piprahwa.

Allen (2012) has now published yet another eminently readable book entitled *Ashoka*, running to some 460 pages. As one journalist has put it, *Ashoka* "humanizes the second century BC emperor in a way that history books have tried and failed"(*Times of India,* 25th March 2012). The title of this book is to some extent a misnomer in so far as, as Allen himself concedes (p.xv), it is as much about the "astonishing tale of painstaking detective work" of the European antiquarian workers as about the words and deeds of Ashoka himself, whom he describes as "a long-forgotten emperor whose song was silenced." Most of the 16 chapters in this book are devoted to the antiquarian studies concerning a variety of Buddhist ruins (edicts, stupas, viharas, pillars, caves, etc.) spread across the country. These studies pertain to the painstaking and prolonged efforts of a series of European workers ranging from Sir William Jones to Francis Buchanan and Colin Mackenzie to James Prinsep and from Alexander Cunningham to John Marshall. References are also made to the late 20th century discoveries of Asokan edicts, such as the ones at Sannati and other places in southern Deccan. The last chapter is a fair assessment of the contents of Ashoka's *dhamma* policy, its rise and eclipse in India due to resurgence of the Brahmanical religion. The book ends with a hope that the new international university coming up at Nalanda may succeed to refocus attention of the world on the wise precepts of Ashoka-*dhamma*. Alongside this widespread public interest, Asoka continues to be a major theme in the academic discourse (Olivelle 2009; Olivelle, Leoshko and Ray 2012).

We now also have some interesting non-specialist writings on more recent periods of Indian history. William Dalrymple is a prominent name among these writers (Fig. 3.7). His two books—*The White Mughals* (2002), and *The Last Mughal* (2006)—while these have been dubbed as pieces of journalistic writing by some historians, have proved to be quite popular among readers, because the facts, personalities and events have been treated in a livelier fashion. Likewise, *Return of a King: The Battle for Afghanistan 1839-1842* (2013) gives a captivating account of the First Anglo-Afghan War and the defeat of

Fig. 3.7 William Dalrymple (1965–), Scottish writer and historian.

the British forces. In his other book entitled *Nine Lives* (2010), Dalrymple has captured how the Indian way of life, despite all modern developments, is still dominated by a large degree of religiosity. The depiction of the past—ancient, medieval and modern—in cinema and on T.V. is a huge topic and many writings exist on it (e.g. Dwyer 2005). Analysis of its effects on the people is a fit topic for detailed investigations in social psychology.

Finally, there is the welcome development of the appearance of non-specialist writings by the Indians themselves about history of Indological studies. Virchand Dharamsey is a senior freelance writer from Mumbai with wide interests ranging from silent cinema to history and participation in archaeological excavations. Based upon his own rich personal archive, he has now published a book-length biography of Bhagwanlal Indraji (1839–1888), a well-known nineteenth-century Indologist of western India (Dharamsey 2012). This book gives a fascinating account of Indraji's contributions to epigraphy, numismatics, art and iconography, religious studies, etc. and also briefs us about his field studies at a host of archaeological sites in western, central and northern India, such as Naneghat, Ajanta, Sanchi, Vidisha and Bodh Gaya (Fig. 3.8).

Fig. 3.8 Bhagwanlal Indraji (1839–1888), the versatile nineteenth-century Indologist of western India.

In conclusion, I wish to restate that dealings with the country's past can no longer be treated as the exclusive domain of academy-based historians and archaeologists. The Indian psyche is sufficiently infused with a sense of the past that literate persons belonging to various groups have felt inspired to write their own accounts and narratives. We stand to learn from the approaches or perspectives adopted by these workers. Kosambi's writings are an excellent example of the attempts to take the study of the past beyond preparation of mere narratives and chronicles of events. It is the society-centred and process-oriented approaches adopted by him that have made his writings very appealing to social scientists. Much earlier, Mahadev Govind Ranade advocated a similar approach for explaining the rise of Maratha power. No less inspiring is Kosambi's emphasis on multidisciplinary perspectives involving archaeology, anthropology and linguistics. There is still much to be accomplished by adopting these approaches. Likewise, the writings of Tagore, Nehru, Amartya Sen and others draw attention to the important fact that a basic knowledge of the country's pluralistic past is absolutely necessary both for understanding the present and for devising plans for future.

We have also considered how even those falling outside the 'read and write' literacy domain arrive at their own versions of the past, stretching from the ancient period to more recent times. These perceptions are not to be evaluated in terms of authenticity and objectivity. Rather one needs to examine the role they play in the day-to-day functioning of the society. The scientific and popular conceptions of the past, while they *prima facie* look antithetic, may finally prove to be complementary. As I wrote elsewhere:

> While the scientific constructions of the past can render the popular versions less fantasy-ridden, more objective and less

amenable to fundamentalist use by vested interests, the popular conceptions could bring in a larger sense of humanism and purpose in truth-finding and objectivity-centered reconstructions of the historians (Paddayya 2011b: 13).

REFERENCES

Allen, Charles. 2002. *The Buddha and the Sahibs.* London: John Murray.

——. 2010. *The Buddha and Dr. Führer: An Archaeological Scandal.* New Delhi: Penguin Books.

——. 2012. *Ashoka.* London: Little Brown.

Bhattacharya, Sabyasachi. 2011a. *Talking Back: The Idea of Civilization in the Indian Nationalist Discourse.* Delhi: Oxford University Press.

——. 2011b. *Rabindranath Tagore: An Interpretation.* New Delhi: Penguin Books.

Chattopadhyaya, B.D. (ed.). 2002. *D.D. Kosambi—Combined Methods in Indology and Other Writings.* Delhi: Oxford University Press.

Chattopadhyaya, D.P. 2001. *The Ways of Understanding the Past: Mythic, Epic, Scientific and Historic.* New Delhi: Centre for Studies in Civilizations.

Clark, J.G.D. 1952. *Prehistoric Europe: The Economic Basis.* London: Methuen.

Cunningham, Alexander. 1871. *Four Reports Made During the Years 1862-63-64-65.* Kolkata: Government Central Press.

Dalrymple, William 2002. *The White Mughals: Love and Betrayal in Eighteenth Century India.* New Delhi: Penguin Books.

——. 2006. *The Last Mughal: The Fall of Delhi, 1857.* New Delhi: Penguin Books.

——. 2010. *Nine Lives: In Search of the Sacred in Modern India.* London: Bloomsbury.

——. 2013. *Return of King: The Battle for Afghanistan 1839-1842.* London: Bloomsbury.

Dharamsey, Virchand. 2012. *Bhagwanlal Indraji—The First Indian Archaeologist: Multidisciplinary Approaches to the Study of the Past.* Vadodara Darshak Itihas Nidhi.

Dhavalikar, M.K. 2008. Professor D.D. Kosambi: The Father of Scientific Indian History. *Bulletin of the Deccan College Research Institute* 66-67: 1-7.

Dwyer, Rachel. 2006. *Filming the Gods—Religion and Indian Cinema.* London: Routledge.

Economic and Political Weekly, A Special Issue on D.D. Kosambi, Volume XLIII, No.30, July 26-August 1, 2008. It contains a set of ten essays written by renowned scholars such as Irfan Habib, Romila Thapar and Sheldon Pollock who assess Kosambi's contributions to various branches of Indology.

Edney, M. 1997. *Mapping an Empire: The Geographical Construction of British India,1765-1843.* Chicago: University of Chicago Press.

Gandhi, M.K. 2006. *Hind Swaraj or Indian Home Rule.* Ahmedabad: Navjivan Publishing House. First published in 1909.

——. 1955. *My Religion* (compiled and edited by Bharatan Kumarappa). Ahmedabad: Navjivan Publishing House.

Gokhale, B.G. 1972. Gandhi and History. *History and Theory* 11: 214-25.

Gokhale, B.G. 1978. Nehru and History. *History and Theory* 17: 311-22.

Gopal, S. 1976. *Jawaharlal Nehru: A Biography* (Volume 1, 1888-1947). New Delhi: Oxford University Press.

Habib, Irfan (ed.). 1974. *Science and Human Progress* (Essays in Humanities, Indology, Science, Mathematics and Personal Tributes to late Prof. Damodar Dharmanand Kosambi). Mumbai: Popular Prakashan.

——. 2001. *Prehistory.* New Delhi: Tulika Books.

——. 2011. *The National Movement: Studies in Ideology and History.* New Delhi: Tulika Books.

Iyer, Raghavan N. 1973. *The Moral and Political Thought of Mahatma Gandhi.* New York: Oxford University Press.

Jha, D.N. (ed.). 2012. *The Many Careers of D.D. Kosambi: Critical Essays.* Delhi: Leftword Books.

Josh, Bhagwan. 2012. Aśoka, Historical Discourse, and the Post-Colonial State. In P. Olivelle, J. Leoshko and H.P. Ray (eds.), *Reimagining Aśoka: Memory and History*, pp. 394-408. New Delhi: Oxford University Press.

Kajale, M.D. 1989. Mesolithic Exploitation of Food Plants in Sri Lanka: Archaeobotanical Study at the Cave Site of Belilena. In D.R. Harris and G.C. Hillman (eds.), *Foraging and Farming: The Evolution of Plant Exploitation*, pp. 269-81. London: Unwin Hyman.

Kajale, M.D. 1996. Plant Resources and Diet Among the Mesolithic Hunters and Foragers. In E. Gennadi Afanas'ev, Serge Cleuziou, John R. Lukas and Maurizio Tosi (eds.), *Colloquium XXXIII: Bioarchaeology of Mesolithic India—An Integrated Approach*, pp. 251-53. Forli, Italy: International Union of Prehistoric and Protohistoric Sciences XIII.

Kakar, Sudhir. 2008. *The Inner World: A Psychoanalytical Study of Childhood and Society in India.* New Delhi: Oxford University Press. Originally published in 1978.

——. 2009. *India Analysed* (Sudhir Kakar in Conversation with Ramin Jahanbegloo). New Delhi: Oxford University Press.

Kakar, Sudhir and Katharina Kakar. 2007. *Indians: Portrait of a People.* New Delhi: Penguin Books.

Kane, P.V. 1930-1962. *History of the Dharmasastras (Ancient and Medieval Religious and Civil Law)*, Volumes I to V. Pune: Bhandarkar Oriental Research Institute.

Katzu, Markandey. 2012. What is India? *Frontline* dated 10 February 2012, pp. 89-97.

Keay, John. 2003. *When Men and Mountains Meet: The Explorers of Western Himalayas 1820-75.* New Delhi: Harper Collins. First published in 1977.

——. 2000a. *The Great Arc: The Dramatic Tale of How India was Mapped and Everest was Named.* London: Harper Collins.

——. 2000b. *India: A History.* London: Harper Perennial.

——. 2001a. *India Discovered: The Recovery of a Lost Civilization.* London: Harper Collins. First published in 1981.

——. 2001b. *The Honourable Company: A History of the British East India Company.* London: Harper Collins.

——. 2011. *To Cherish and Conserve: The Early Years of the Archaeological Survey of India.* New Delhi: Archaeological Survey of India and National Culture Fund.

Keyuing, Wijze. 2011. *Ashoka the Great.* (Translated from Dutch by J.E. Steur). Mumbai: Rupa & Co.

Kirtikar, Vasudeva J. 1924. *Studies in Vedanta.* Mumbai: D.B. Taraporevala and Sons.

Kosambi, D.D. 1956. *Introduction to the Study of Indian History.* Mumbai: Popular Prakashan.

——. 1957. *Exasperating Essays: Exercises in Dialectical Method.* Pune: Popular Book House.

——. 1962. *Myth and Reality.* Mumbai: Popular Prakashan.

——. 1965. *The Culture and Civilization of Ancient India in Historical Outline.* London: Routledge.

——. 1972. Adventures into the Unknown. In K. Satchidananda Murty and B. Ramakrishna Rao (eds.), *Current Trends in Indian Philosophy*, pp. 158-9. Waltair: Asia Publishing House. As quoted by B.D. Chattopadhyaya (2002: xiv).

Misra, V.N. 1990. The Van Vagris: 'Lost' Hunters of the Thar Desert, Rajasthan. *Man and Environment* 15(2): 89-108.

Murty, M.L.K. 1981. Hunter-Gatherer Ecosystems and Archaeological Patterns of Subsistence Behaviour on the Southeast Coast of India: An Ethnographic Model. *World Archaeology* 12: 47-58.

——. 1985. Ethnoarchaeology of the Kurnool Cave Areas, South India. *World Archaeology* 17(2): 192-205.
Nandy, Ashis. 2002. History's Forgotten Doubles. In *Romance of the State and the Fate of Dissent in the Tropics* (Ashis Nandy), pp. 83-109. Originally published in *History and Theory* 34(1985): 44-66.
Nehru, Jawaharlal. 1993. *Letters from a Father to his Daughter.* Kolkata: Oxford University Press. Fifty-ninth Impression. First published in 1931.
——. 1960. *The Discovery of India.* London: Meridian Books.
——. 1962. *Glimpses of World History.* Mumbai: Asia Publishing House. Originally published in 1934-35.
Olivelle, P. (ed.). 2009. *Asoka in History and Historical Memory.* New Delhi: Motilal Banarasidass.
Olivelle, P., J. Leoshko and H.P. Ray (eds.). 2012. *Reimagining Aśoka: Memory and History.* New Delhi: Oxford University Press.
Paddayya, K. 1978. New Research Designs and Field Techniques in the Palaeolithic Archaeology of India. *World Archaeology* 10: 94-110.
——. 1979. Palaeoethnography *vis-à-vis* the Stone Age Cultures of India: Some Methodological Considerations. *Bulletin of the Deccan College Research Institute* 38(1978-79): 63-90.
——. 1982. *The Acheulian Culture of the Hunsgi Valley (Peninsular India): ASettlement System Perspective.* Pune: Deccan College.
——. 2008. South Asia: Palaeolithic Cultures. In D.M. Pearsall (ed.), *Encyclopaedia of Archaeology,* Volume 1, pp. 768-91. Oxford: Elsevier and Academic Press.
——. 2010. Excavation at Acheulian Locality VI near Yediyapur, Baichbal Valley, Karnataka. *Bulletin of the Deccan College Research Institute* 66-67 (2006-07): 95-111.
——. 2011a. Stone Age Technology in India. *Ancient India* (New Series) 1: 9-68.

——. 2011b. The Place of the Past in the Indian Mind. *Journal of the Asiatic Society* (Kolkata) 53: 1-18.

Pal, Bipin Chandra. 2000. *The Soul of India: A Constructive Study of Indian Thought and Ideals.* New Delhi: Rupa & Co.

Parekh, Bhikhu. 1995. *Gandhi's Political Philosophy.* Delhi.

Pathak, V.S. 1966. *Ancient Historians of India: A Study in Historical Biographies*. Mumbai: Asia Publishing House.

Phillimore, R.H. 1945-54. *Historical Records of the Survey of India,* Volumes I to III. Dehra Dun: Survey of India.

Raju, D.R. 1988. *Stone Age Hunter-Gatherers: An Ethnoarchaeology of Cuddapah Region, Southeast India.* Pune: Ravish Publishers.

Ranade, Mahadev Govind. 1961. *Rise of Maratha Power*. New Delhi: Publications Division, Government of India. First published in 1900.

Ranade, R.D. 2001. *Essays and Reflections* (Compiled by B.R. Kulkarni). Mumbai: Bharatiya Vidya Bhavan. First published in 1964.

Ray, H.P. 2008. *Colonial Archaeology in South Asia: The Legacy of Sir Mortimer Wheeler.* Delhi: Oxford University Press.

Rich, Bruce. 2008. *To Uphold the World: The Message of Ashoka and Kautilya for the 21st Century.* New Delhi: Penguin Books.

Sen, Amartya. 1996a. *On Interpreting India's Past.* Kolkata: Asiatic Society.

——. 1996b. Taking Pride in a Pluralistic Society. *Span* (June-July 1996): 8-11, 22-23.

——. 1999. *Development as Freedom*. New Delhi: Oxford University Press.

——. 2001. History and the Enterprise of Knowledge. Inaugural Address at the 61st Annual Session of Indian History Congress, January 2001, Kolkata.

Sengupta, G., S. Roychoudhary and S. Som (ed.). 2006. *Past and Present: Ethnoarchaeology in India.* New Delhi: Pragati Publications and Kolkata: Centre for Archaeological Studies and Training, Eastern India.

Sharma, Arvind. 2003. *Hinduism and Its Sense of History.* Delhi: Oxford University Press.

Sharma, R.S. (ed.). 1974. *Indian Society: Historical Probings in Memory of D.D. Kosambi:* New Delhi: People's Publishing House.

Thapar, Romila. 1984. *Ancient Indian Social History: Some Interpretations.* Hyderabad: Orient Longman.

——. 1991. Genealogical Patterns as Perceptions of the Past. *Studies in History* 7: 1-36.

——. 1992. *Interpreting Early India.* Delhi: Oxford University Press.

——. 2013. *The Past Before Us—Historical Traditions of Early North India.* Ranikhet: Permanent Black.

Tilak, B.G. 1903. *Arctic Home in the Vedas.* Pune: Manager, Kesari Press.

——. 1935-36. *Srimad Bhagavadgita Rahasya,* Volumes I and II (Translated into English by B.S. Sukthankar). Mumbai: Bombay Vaibhav Press.

Wheeler, R.E.M. 1960. *Early India and Pakistan.* London: Thames and Hudson.

CHAPTER IV

Darwinian Revolution and the Birth of Prehistory

INTRODUCTION

The core ideas of the evolution of living organisms involving the processes of constant striving and survival of the fitter ones were jointly presented by Charles Darwin and his compatriot Alfred Wallace before the Linnean Society in 1858 (Fig. 4.1). In November the following year, Darwin published his findings as a lengthy Abstract entitled *On the Origin of Species*, embodying the results of his two-decade-long work in natural history (Darwin 1970). Darwin thus introduced into the world of scientific thought a conceptual framework which, like the Copernican heliocentric theory, William Harvey's theory of blood circulation, Newtonian gravitation theory and Charles Lyell's theory of the origin of earth, fundamentally altered man's perception of the nature of phenomenal world and its functioning. As expected, the theory of evolution exercised enormous influence on subsequent thought in both natural and social sciences. In social life too capitalists, communists and the Nazis invoked, wrongly of course, some of the ideas of Darwin to justify their own theories of society, so much so that Darwin came to be considered as the most dangerous man.

Fig. 4.1 Charles Darwin (1809–1882), author of *On the Origin of Species.*

Darwin captured the essence of the theory of evolution in elegant words in the concluding paragraph of *On the Origin of Species*:

> ...It is interesting to contemplate an entangled bank clothed with many plants of many kinds, with birds singing on the bushes, with various insects flitting about, and with worms crawling through the damp earth, and to reflect that these elaborately constructed forms, so different from each other, and dependent on each other in so complex a manner, have all been produced by laws acting around us. These laws, taken in the largest sense, being Growth with Reproduction; Inheritance which is almost implied by Reproduction; Variability from the indirect and direct action of the external conditions of life, and from use and disuse; a Ratio of Increase so high as to lead to a Struggle for life and as a consequence to Natural Selection, entailing Divergence of Character and the extinction of less improved forms. Thus, from the war of nature, from famine and death, the most exalted object which we are capable of conceiving, namely, the production of higher animals, directly follows. There is grandeur in this view of life, with its several powers, having been originally breathed into a few forms or into one; and that, while this planet has gone cycling on according to the fixed law of

> gravity, from so simple a beginning endless forms most beautiful and most wonderful have been, and are being, evolved (Darwin 1970: 459-60).

Much praise has since been showered on this paragraph both for its scientific spirit and for its poetical and philosophical attitudes of mind (Dawkins 2010: 397-426).

Underlying the theory of evolution, there are certain simple but very important ideas:

1. God is deleted from the topic of emergence of life
2. Nor was there any design and planning in the emergence of life; it was a matter of chance.
3. Immense amount of time is involved in the process of development of life forms.
4. Organisms are not static but are always striving and amenable to change.
5. Out of this striving, new and different/improved forms of life appear.

Darwin graciously acknowledged his debt to the ideas of many previous writers (Darwin 1970: 53-63). Almost all of them were naturalists (geologists or palaeontologists or plant and animal scientists) or plant- and animal-breeders of the 18th and 19th centuries. In this chapter, I wish to point out that the germs of several of the principal notions constituting Darwin's theory could be traced to the writings of many other thinkers stretching back to the ancient period. In particular, there are four categories of thought which deserve mention, viz., philosophical thought, social thought, religious thought and antiquarian studies. After a brief survey of these streams of thought, I will point out how the theory of evolution served as a source of strength to the newly recognized discipline of prehistory. We will conclude with a few remarks about how these developments in Europe inspired the birth of Indian prehistory. I should perhaps clarify at this stage that it is not the intent of this essay to shake the high pedestal which Darwin occupies in the history of scientific thought. It only seeks to emphasize the fertility of human mind irrespective of its temporal placement and that the topic of history of ideas is of absorbing interest.

PROCESS PHILOSOPHY

Process philosophy is one of the principal schools of human thought. Temporality, historicity, change and passage are its fundamental components (Rescher 2000: 6). In modern philosophy, it is often associated with A.N. Whitehead. But, as pointed out by Rescher (2000: 3-5), process philosophy has long historical roots.

Since the days of Aristotle, Western metaphysics showed a bias in favour of things *per se*. Aristotle provided for a metaphysical centrality to the principle of primacy of substances. Parminides expressed it well when he said that "Nature consists of the changeable interrelations among stable, unchangeable units of existence." But pre-Socratic philosophy laid emphasis on another category, viz., processes, events and recurrences. Its leading exponent was Heraclitus, who made the famous statement: "All things flow." Process was held as fundamental. For example, a river is not an object but a continuous flow. Nor is the sun a thing but an enduring fire.

The Latin poet Lucretius, more than 2000 years ago, in his famous poem *De Rerum Natura (On the Nature of Things)* ignored God and visualized the world in evolutionary terms (Lucretius 1886). In his view, the beginning of universe took place not by design but through chance collisions of atoms.

Fig. 4.2 Gottfried Wilhelm von Leibniz (1646–1716), a noted German thinker and philosopher.

Immense amount of time was involved in this process. He also envisioned that nature creates all things, fosters them and finally dissolves them into itself when they perish. Even more significantly, Lucretius held that the essence of development lay in a number of natural experiments, as a result of which some forms of life survived and the weaker ones were weeded out. Thus, the basic ideas of struggle and adaptation were already hinted at by Lucretius.

The 17th century German philosopher Gottfried Leibniz was the first major exponent of process view in modern Western philosophy (Fig. 4.2). He held that all things which figure in our experience are not substances but mere phenomena. The world consists of clusters of processes which he designated as monads. Leibniz saw in nature a unity of diversified things. The law of continuity ensuing from the unity and multiplicity of things governs all change. Also noteworthy is his principle of appetition, i.e., striving, through which all things endeavour to bring forth new features.

A.N. Whitehead developed the concept of process philosophy in an elaborate way (Fig. 4.3). In his book *Science and the Modern World*, Whitehead wrote: "Thus nature is a structure of evolving process. The reality is the process" (Whitehead 1975:92). Likewise, in *Adventure of Ideas* he stated: "One principle is that the very essence of real actuality—that is, of the completely real—is *process* (*sic*). Thus, each actual thing is only to be understood in terms of its becoming and perishing..." (Whitehead 1933: 354).

Fig. 4.3 Alfred North Whitehead (1861–1947), a noted British philosopher and thinker.

Whitehead developed his ideas of process in an elaborate way in the Gifford Lectures which he delivered at the University of Edinburgh in 1927-28; these were published in 1929 as a book entitled *Process and Reality* (Whitehead 1985). He magnanimously refers to the writings of earlier philosophers like Heni Bergson, Bertrand Russell, John Dewey and C.S. Peirce. Whitehead builds upon Bergson's notion of nature as process and seeks to replace traditional philosophy of substance with the philosophy of organism, which alone can provide clarification of a universe in which process, dynamic actualization, interdependence and creativity are disclosed as the primary data of immediate experience. In his own words:

> Each actual entity is itself only describable as an organic process. It repeats in microcosm what the universe is in macrocosm. It is a process proceeding from phase to phase, each phase being the real basis from which its successor proceeds towards the completion of the thing in question. (Whitehead 1985: 215).

For this purpose Whitehead proposes the method of descriptive generalization which takes the form of a description of dynamic process rather than of static structure.

SOCIAL THOUGHT

In social thought, attention should in particular be drawn to the concept or idea of progress, postulating development of human society from a simple stage to a more evolved or complex level. For an early statement on this concept, we have once again to go back to the poet Lucretius. Probably influenced by the ideas of Democritus and other Greek writers, and also based upon the use of reason and informed speculation, Lucretius proposed that the earth first gave birth to all kinds of herbage, then to all races of mortal creatures, and then to races of mortal men. He then went on to say that for a long time men led the life of roving beasts, with no knowledge of either plough or planting of seeds or use of iron. They dwelled in woods and subsisted on wild plants and hunting of animals with stone tools and clubs. Slowly they got acquainted with the use of fire and skins for clothing, and construction of huts. Then came the use of iron and practices of tillage and planting of saplings. This stage was followed by the formation of social relationships and development of religion and language. Lucretius is therefore regarded as the progenitor of the 19th century Three-Age System in archaeology.

The early or classical Greek thought provided for the conception of natural growth of knowledge (arts and science) and advance of human condition. Disagreeing with the views of John Bury (1928), Nisbert maintains that the concept of progress continued into the early Christian thought and Mediaeval period (Nisbert 1980: x). The early Christian thought, starting from Eusebius and Tertullian and reaching up to the works of St.

Augustine, added to the concept of progress some new attributes, which in turn introduced a spiritual dimension. These attributes included the vision of the unity of all mankind, role of historical necessity, progress as the unfolding of a design through long ages, and gradual spiritual perfection of mankind (Nisbert 1980: 47-76).

The idea of progress further got elaborated in the works of various writers during the period 1600 to 1850, which also covers the Age of Enlightenment (Becker and Barnes 1961: 458-506). One of the general notions advocated was that contemporary civilization developed from a lower level. Bacon proposed that the present generation was wiser than previous ones. Kant advocated progress of mankind in terms of morality. Condorcet postulated that human history passed through ten great epochs, of which the first stages were hunting and fishing and animal domestication.

A true combination of precocity and profound understanding is to be found in the lecture on "Successive Advances of the Human Mind" delivered by the 24-year-old Frenchman Turgot at the Sorbonne in 1750 (Fig. 4.4). In this lecture Turgot advocated the notion of physical unity of mankind, but he provided for a great diversity of customs and institutions. Secondly, he remarked that mankind presents an overvaried spectacle of progress from infancy to maturity. He postulated mankind's passage through the three important and successive stages of barbarism, agriculture and civilization. Similar ideas were put forward by Adam Ferguson, William Robertson and other thinkers of the Scottish Enlightenment (Garrett 2003). It is very probable that Gordon Childe was influenced by the Enlightenment ideas like these for periodization of prehistory into Palaeolithic savagery, Neolithic barbarism and urban revolution in his famous books *Man Makes Himself* (1936) and *What Happened in History* (1942).

Fig. 4.4 Anne Robert Jacques Turgot (1727–1781), a noted French thinker of the Age of Enlightenment.

Then there are the views of some 19th century social scientists who are rightly or wrongly called Social Darwinists. Among these, the views of two writers deserve mention. John Malthus's work, *An Essay on the Principle of Population*, published in 1798, was obviously influenced by the effects of Industrial Revolution. Malthus therefore reacted against the optimistic views expressed about the human society by earlier workers like Condorcet. He postulated a tendency for the population to grow beyond the means of subsistence. This in turn leads to an unrelenting struggle for the bare means of existence, in which process the weaker ones are eliminated. Darwin had the benefit of reading this essay before the publication of *On the Origin of Species* and in fact makes a reference to it to this effect (Darwin 1970: 68). The other writer is Herbert Spencer, who was for some time the chief engineer of British railroad construction. Improving upon the ideas of August Comte who had postulated the passage of Social Science through theological, metaphysical and positive or scientific stages, Spencer developed the organismic theory of human society in his book *Social Statics* published in 1850, i.e., nearly a decade prior to the publication of Darwin's own book. Here, Spencer pointed out that many analogies exist between human society and organisms. For example, both show growth and increase in size and complexity, unlike inorganic matter. In both cases structural and functional differentiation takes place. And the general law of evolution is applicable to social organisms too (for details, see Becker and Barnes 1961: 664-92).

In the 20th century social science, there were some important efforts to introduce the concept of process in order to understand the functional interrelations among the components of social systems. Arthur Bentley's book *The Process of Government* (1949) concerns political science and was greatly influenced by the writings of two Germanic thinkers in sociology, George Simmel and Max Weber (Kress 1970). Functionalism in anthropology, which came up in the middle of the century, was another important development connected with process-oriented view of reality (Harris 1968: 514-67).

RELIGIOUS THOUGHT

Christian theology provided for a short chronology for the history of earth and man. In the 17th century Archbishop Ussehr and Bishop Lightfoot, based upon the calculations given in *Genesis*, arrived at the date of 4004 BC for the origin of world and man. This chronology was widely accepted in the Christian world (Daniel 1967: 110). As against this, oriental religions provided for a much longer duration. For example, ancient Hindu thought viewed time as imperishable. The concept of *Mahayuga* (Great Cycle) consists of four *yugas* and covers 4,320,000 years. The *Mahayuga* ends in destruction by fire and flood, and is followed by another Great Cycle and so on. Charles Lyell, the founder of modern geology, invoked ideas from Hindu mythology in his book *Principles of Geology*. While explaining the process of evolution, he made a reference to the Hindu trinity of Gods and their powers—Brahma the creator, Vishnu the preserver and Shiva the destroyer (Gould 1991: 171). In this connection, reference may also be made to the concept of ten *avataras* of Vishnu—some taking animal forms and some human—all emphasizing the basic unity and continuity of life forms.

ANTIQUARIAN STUDIES

The fourth strand of thought concerns antiquarian studies. It is well known that C.J. Thomsen, the curator of the Royal Danish Museum in Copenhagen, made the first systematic attempt at temporal partitioning of the pre-Christian past of Northern Europe. Confronted as he was with the task of organizing a variegated collection of artefacts of different materials that had accumulated in the museum, he used ideas taken from ethnographic sources and also observations of Enlightenment thinkers and embarked upon a detailed cataloguing of the objects—their shapes and raw materials, edge- or non-edge forms, etc. This laborious museum work emboldened Thomsen to put forward the famous Three-Age System in 1836 (Paddayya 1993). That is, the pre-Christian past of Northern Europe consisted of three stages, viz., the Stone, Bronze

Fig. 4.5 Christian Jurgensen Thomsen (1788–1865), the Curator of the Royal Danish Museum in Copenhagen, who developed Three-Age System for studying the preliterate past.

and Iron Ages (Fig. 4.5). It was for the first time that the preliterate record of man was taken serious note of and divided into three successive stages. It was presumed that the duration covered by these stages was still within the 6000-year long chronological framework accepted by Christian theology. Soon this periodisation postulating progress of human culture was verified stratigraphically in the excavations conducted in the Danish peatbogs by Thomsen's assistant J.J. Worsaae. Indeed, the Three-Age System served as the cornerstone of modern archaeology and led to many rapid developments in prehistory. It definitely introduced the *logos* component into antiquarian studies.

ANTIQUITY OF MAN

As regards the temporal duration of Stone Age, it is a matter of happy coincidence that from about the time of announcement of the Three-Age System in 1836, the French customs official Boucher de Perthes started finding very primitive stone implements along with mammalian fossil fauna in the gravels of the river Somme in France at Abbeville and other places. He claimed that these implements, associated as they were with ancient gravels as well as fossil fauna, dated to the Ice Age, thereby stretching human antiquity to a remote period. While these findings did not invite any favourbale

Fig. 4.6 John Frere (1740–1807), the British antiquary who identified the first ever true Palaeolithic site at Hoxne in Suffolk (England) in 1797.

response within France itself, they did excite the attention of British workers. Joseph Prestwich and Charles Lyell (both geologists), Hugh Falconer (palaeontologist) and John Evans (archaeologist) made two or three visits to France in 1859. Prestwich's visit to France rekindled in him interest in the finding of stone tools that had been made at Hoxne in England by John Frere in 1797 (Frere 1800) and he therefore made it a point to visit this site (Figs. 4.6-4.8). Against this background of personal inspection of actual sites, Prestwich read his famous paper before the Royal Society in London on 26 May 1859 and ratified the French and British findings (Fig. 4.9). This is the celebrated paper which led to the birth of prehistory (Prestwich 1860). It was accepted that the flint pieces from France and Hoxne were made by men who lived in a remote period along with wild mammals and that the surface of the area they occupied had not yet acquired

Fig. 4.7 Flint handaxe found by John Frere at Hoxne in 1797.

Fig. 4.8 Jacques Boucher de Crevecoeur de Perthes (1788–1868), the French customs official who found prehistoric implements and fossil fauna in the drift gravels of Somme valley in northern France in the 1830s and 1840s.

Fig. 4.9 Sir Joseph Prestwich (1812–1896), the British geologist who upheld the findings of John Frere and Boucher de Perthes before the Royal Society (London) in May 1859.

the present shape. A week later, John Evans made a similar announcement about these findings at the Society of Antiquaries, London (Evans 1860). What is important to note is that the announcements of Prestwich and Evans preceded by five months the publication of Darwin's book *On the Origin of Species.*

The publication of *On the Origin of Species* and Darwin's other book *The Descent of Man* in 1871 gave real stimulus to prehistoric studies. In his book *Prehistoric Times* published in 1865, John Lubbock divided the Stone Age into Palaeolithic and Neolithic stages. What is even more remarkable, the various discoveries in England, France and other West European countries in the next two decades made it possible to arrive at a finer division of the Palaeolithic into Lower, Middle and Upper Palaeolithic stages, the latter with several sub-stages. Further, a transitional stage called the Mesolithic was recognized between the Palaeolithic and Neolithic periods. All these developments led to the establishment of a full-fledged prehistoric culture-sequence by the end of the 19th century (for details, see Daniel 1964).

Birth of Indian Prehistory

It is equally remarkable that prehistoric studies were initiated in India close on the heels of their birth in Europe. The credit for this goes to Robert Bruce Foote, one of the officers of the Geological Survey of India (Chakrabarti 1989; Paddayya 2009). He found implements of the Palaeolithic in a lateritic gravel pit at Pallavaram near Chennai on 30 May 1863 and followed it up with the discovery of over 400 prehistoric sites in different parts of south India in the next two decades (Fig. 4.10). Foote was clearly inspired by the epoch-making discoveries that were being made in Europe. In his own words:

Fig. 4.10 Robert Bruce Foote (1834–1912) of the Geological Survey of India, Father of Indian prehistory.

In the early sixties of last century every one interested in the origin of mankind had been greatly stirred by the thorough confirmation by the English geologists, Joseph Prestwich, John Evans, and Hugh Falconer, of Boucher de Perthes' discovery in the drift beds of the Somme river valley of chipped flint implements, the earliest human artifacts then known. The news of

> this remarkable revelation had turned my thoughts, to the necessity of looking out for possible similar traces of early human art in South India where my work then lay... (Foote 1916: v).

Although Foote does not make a specific reference, it is most likely that Foote's discoveries were also influenced by the publication of Darwin's book *On the Origin of Species* and the complete transformation it brought about in man's ideas about the development of organic life. The reason is that Charles Lyell, the founder of geology to which Foote also belonged, was actively involved in defending the theory of evolution in the European circles in the 1860s.

Foote not only made careful collections of various kinds of cultural material from the Indian sites but undertook a systematic study of the objects and prepared two detailed catalogues (Foote 1914; 1916). He grouped the sites into three periods, viz., Palaeolithic, Neolithic and Iron Age. As concerns the Palaeolithic period, he made some pertinent observations about the distribution of sites and their correlation with natural vegetation, rainfall and raw material availability (Foote 1916: 1-46). He contributed several papers on his prehistoric findings to some Indian periodicals and also took steps to publish articles in British journals like *Geological Magazine* and *Journal of the Geological Society of London*. He participated in conferences in London, Vienna and other places and even exhibited some of the Indian specimens on these occasions. These exhibitions created a very good impression about the similarities between the Indian and European bifacial implements. And a reference was made to the Indian implements in the general works dealing with stone tools from Europe (Evans 1872: 570). For his manifold contributions, Foote is rightly called the Father of Indian Prehistory. It is

Fig. 4.11 James Fergusson (1808-1886), who pioneered the study of building architecture of ancient and medieval India.

important to realize that his discoveries in India were made at a time when Africa was still unheard of in prehistoric studies.

It appears that the Darwinian ideas also influenced other branches of Indian studies. For instance, we can cite James Fergusson's study of ancient Indian temple architecture (Fig. 4.11). Fergusson came to India as a businessman and indigo-planter but was soon fascinated by its ancient temples. Between 1829 and 1847, he undertook extensive architectural surveys in different parts of the country, involving preparation of careful notes, drawing of sketches and making of plans. After returning to England he published two major volumes (Fergusson 1845, 1876) and also gave public lectures on this topic. He grouped the Indian temples into Hindu, Buddhist, Jain and Muslim periods, and identified several developmental stages in building construction—Dravidian, Indo-Aryan, Himalayan, Mughal, Rajput, etc. After listening to one of these lectures, T.H. Huxley wondered whether Darwinismus had not percolated fields where "You least expected it" (as quoted by Allchin 1961: 242). John Dewey (1997) drew attention to the influence of Darwinian thought on the development of philosophy (see also Appleman 1979; Bowler 1990).

Evolutionary archaeology, incorporating Darwinian ideas, has emerged as a prominent trend in archaeology since 1980s. Following upon the earlier perspectives of group adaptation and cultural selectionism, more recent themes have focused on the individual; interaction between biological and cultural modes of inheritance; and cognitive approach to human psychology. The topics dealt with range from development of stone technology to art to social inequality (for a general review, see Maschner 1996; O'Brien and Lyman 2000).

REFERENCES

Allchin, F.R. 1961. Ideas of History in Indian Historical Writings: A Preliminary Study. In C.H. Philips (ed.), *Historians of India, Pakistan and Ceylon*, pp. 241-59. London: Oxford University Press.

Appleman, P. 1979. *Darwin: A Norton Critical Edition*. New York: W.W. Norton & Company.

Becker, H. and H.E. Barnes. 1961. *Social Thought from Lore to Science*, Volume 2. New York: Dover Publications, Inc. First published in 1938 by D.C. Heath and Company.

Bentley, A.F. 1949. *The Process of Government*. Evanston, Illinois: Principia Press.

Bowler, Peter J. 1990. *Charles Darwin: The Man and His Influence*. Oxford: Basil Blackwell.

Bury, J.B. 1928. *The Idea of Progress: An Inquiry into its Origins and Growth*. London: Macmillan and Co.

Chakrabarti, D.K. 1979. Robert Bruce Foote and Indian Prehistory. *East and West* 29: 11-26.

Childe, V.G. 1936. *Man Makes Himself*. London: Watts and Co.

——. 1942. *What Happened in History*. Harmondsworth: Penguin Books Ltd.

Daniel, Glyn. 1964. *The Idea of Prehistory*. Harmondsworth: Penguin Books Ltd.

——. 1967. *The Origins and Growth of Archaeology.* Harmondsworth: Penguin Books Ltd.

Darwin, Charles. 1970. *On the Origin of Species by Means of Natural Selection or The Preservation of Favoured Races in the Struggle for Life.* Harmondsworth: Penguin Books Ltd. First published in 1859 by John Murray, London.

——. 1871. *The Descent of Man and Selection in Relation to Sex.* London: John Murray.

Dawkins, Richard. 2010. *The Greatest Show on Earth: The Evidence for Evolution.* London: Random House Company.

Dewey, John. 1997. The Influence of Darwinism on Philosophy, in John Dewey, *The Influence of Darwin on Philosophy and Other Essays,* pp. 1-19. New York: Prometheus Books. Originally published in 1907.

Evans, John. 1860. On the Occurrence of Flint Implements in Undisturbed Beds of Gravel and Clay. *Archaeologia* 38: 180.

——. 1872. *The Ancient Stone Implements, Weapons and Ornaments of Great Britain.* London: Longman, Green, Reader and Ryder.

Foote, R.B. 1914. *The Foote Collection of Indian Prehistoric and Protohistoric Antiquities: Catalogue Raisonne.* Chennai: Government Museum.

Foote, R.B. 1916. *The Foote Collection of Indian Prehistoric and Protohistoric Antiquities: Notes on their Ages and Distribution.* Chennai: Government Museum.

Frere, John. 1800. Account of Flint Implements Discovered at Hoxne in Suffolk. *Archaeologia* 13: 204-05.

Garrett, A. 2003. Anthropology: The Origins of Human Nature. In A. Broadie (ed.), *The Scottish Enlightenment,* pp. 79-93. Cambridge: Cambridge University Press.

Gould, S.J. 1988. *Time's Arrow, Time's Cycle: Myth and Metaphor in the Discovery of Geological Time.* Harmondsworth: Penguin Books Ltd.

Harris, Marvin. 1968. *The Rise of Anthropological Theory: A History of Theories of Culture.* London: Routledge & Kegan Paul Ltd.

Kress, P.A. 1970. *Social Science and the Idea of Process: The Ambiguous Legacy of Arthur F. Bentley*. Urbana: University of Illinois Press.

Lucretius. 1886. *On the Nature of Things* (Translation of *De Rerum Natura* by H.A.J. Munro). Cambridge: Dreighton Bell and Co.

Maschner, H.D.G. (ed.). 1996. *Darwinian Archaeologies*. New York: Plenum Press.

Nisbet, R. 1980. *History of the Idea of Progress*. New York: Basic Books.

O'Brien, M.J. and R.L. Lyman (ed.). 2000. *Applying Evolutionary Archaeology: A Systematic Approach*. New York: Kluwer Academic/Plenum Publishers.

Paddayya, K. 1993. C.J. Thomsen and the Three Age System. *Man and Environment* 18(2): 129-40.

——. 2009. Contributions of Robert Bruce Foote to Indian Prehistory. In K. Paddayya, P.P. Joglekar, K.K. Basa and R. Sawant (eds.), *Recent Research Trends in South Asian Archaeology* (Proceedings of the Professor H.D. Sankalia Birth Centenary Seminar), pp. 171-80. Pune: Deccan College.

Prestwich, Joseph. 1860. On the Occurrence of Flint Implements, Associated with the Remains of Extinct Mammalia, in the Undisturbed Beds of a Late Geological Period. *Proceedings of the Royal Society* (London) 10: 50-59.

Rescher, N. 2000.*Process Philosophy: A Survey of Basic Issues*. Pittsburgh: University of Pittsburgh Press.

Whitehead, A.N. 1975. *Science and the Modern World*. Glasgow: William Collins Sons Co. Ltd. Originally published in 1926 by Cambridge University Press, Cambridge.

——. 1933. *Adventure of Ideas*. London: Cambridge University Press.

——. 1985. *Process and Reality* (Corrected Edition by D.R. Griffin and D.W. Sherburne). New York: The Free Press. Originally published in 1929 by Cambridge University Press, Cambridge.

CHAPTER V

The Past in the Indian Mind

INTRODUCTION

According to geographers, the best starting point for any study of the river Ganges is its origin in the Himalayas. Sir William Jones is our reference point in Oriental studies. In tune with the spirit of the Age of Enlightenment to which he belonged, Sir William, within less than half a year after assuming charge as a puisne judge of the East India Company's Supreme Court at Kolkata, founded The Asiatic Society in 1784 with the noble aim of investigating the Oriental lands—their geographies, histories, antiquities, religions, philosophies, languages and literatures, sciences, cultures, etc. It is well known that Sir William mastered Sanskrit within a few years after his arrival in India and used this language proficiency as a means for writing on a variety of Indological topics covering philosophy, religion, fine arts, history and other branches.

The Asiatic Society served as the springboard for all natural and humanistic disciplines in India. Beginning with these foundations, Indological studies have progressed over the last two centuries and a quarter. All Indological disciplines devoted to the study of India's heritage—languages, culture, archaeology, history, religion and philosophy—have established identities of their own in terms of subject matter, aims and goals, method and theory. The scope of this essay is by and large confined to ancient Indian history and archaeology.

It is surely a sign of the high level of academic maturity attained by these two disciplines that they have experienced first-rate debates about general epistemological issues. In the realm of ancient Indian history, colonial perceptions were followed by nationalist trends in the decades immediately after Independence. Soon, more than one trend in the application of Marxist notions of theory and method in history also cropped up. Trends like the *Annales* school endeavoured to introduce canons of the scientific method into history-writing and replace emphasis on reconstruction of political history by a concern with socio-economic aspects of past societies. Subaltern studies sought to highlight the role of lower order groups in the development of historical societies (Thapar 1968; 2002: 3-20, 74-94).

Paradigm shifts took place in Indian archaeology too. Till the 1970s, framing of culture-history and reconstruction of past lifeways were the main objectives in Indian archaeology; these are no doubt valid even today. But since the 1970s new perspectives began to be introduced—first, the rise of processual archaeology advocating the cause of inferring human behaviour from archaeological record and then, from the 1990s, the growth of what are called ideational trends highlighting the need to recover the human minds generating behaviour. All these perspectives have introduced a lively debate in Indian archaeology (Paddayya 2002a).

Historiographical studies too have experienced quite an amount of stir in respect of overall perspectives. Post-modernism was formally introduced in Oriental studies with the publication of Edward Said's book *Orientalism* in 1978. Said indicted Western scholarship in Oriental studies as a discourse meant for promoting the interests of colonial regimes. Orientalism was

> the corporate institution for dealing with the Orient—dealing with it by making statements about it; ruling over it; in short, Orientalism as a Western style for dominating, restructuring and having authority over the Orient (Said 1978: 3).

Taking cue from this starting point, Inden and other writers argued that there was a need to develop indigenist perspectives for understanding ancient Indian culture and society (Inden 1990). At the same time, critical editions of the epics *Mahabharata* and *Ramayana* have been treated by Western scholars "as part of the Hindu nationalist endeavour to nationalize the past" (van der Veer 1999). The book *Colonial Indology* by Chakrabarti (1997) offers a strongly worded critique of colonial perspectives in Indian studies. More recently, he has published a new book entitled *The Battle for Ancient India* (Chakrabarti 2009).

There is no doubt that some amount of truth exists in all these criticisms about Western scholarship in Indological studies. But it is also important to realize that there is some wisdom in the exhortation made by Daniel Ingalls (1960: 107) half a century ago:

> The motives for studying the past seem to me as various as motives of humans for any other endeavour.... Let us be thankful for man's infinite variety and, instead of arguing about the approaches and motives of scholarship, concentrate our criticism on the results. On the results, I think, we will find ourselves essentially in agreement.

Notwithstanding these developments in Indological studies, there are many aspects concerning both substantive content and theory and method, which need focused attention in the decades to come. Secondly, I wish to argue that there is a large gap in our understanding of the sociological dimension of heritage studies in India. It is contended here that, while one must applaud the sincere efforts made over the last two hundred years and more to reconstruct the past from material and non-material (archaeological and literary) sources, adequate attention has not been paid to the fact that India is one of the ancient regions of the world where the interest in the past is not confined to academic corridors alone but runs much deeper in society. There are vast sections of people which, though they have never touched the portals of educational institutions and therefore lack 'read and write' literacy, have not merely imbibed a deep sense of the past but in fact draw upon it in conducting their daily lives. While we as Indologists are students of the past, common people in India are, to borrow a phrase from the psychoanalyst Ivan Illich (as quoted in Nandy 2002: 102), students of the pastness itself. Indeed, the past has become an inalienable part of the Indian ethos or cultural gene pool. A major research project in social psychology is required to understand the nature and use of sense of the past prevalent among the Indian people and its use in day-to-day life. Let us make today a small attempt in this direction.

THE INDIAN MIND

Any consideration of the imprint made by the past on society has to commence with an understanding of the basic nature of the Indian mind. Following upon a long preliterate past spanning one million years and beyond, India has a recorded history of about four thousand years. During this period the country witnessed many intrusions, invasions and convulsions but the basic character of Indian identity or ethos has not changed in any drastic way and often the influences received from outside have been smoothly amalgamated into the pre-existing scheme of things. If one may ignore some likely mild protests to the contrary, what is called the Indian identity is basically Hindu in character with later accretions derived from the Buddhist, Jain, Muslim and colonial sources, all blended together harmoniously over a long period of time. Nehru (1960) called India a palimpsest of cultural layers. While this much is clear about the long chronology and composite character of the Indian identity, various writers have given their own interpretations of its constituent elements. The following readings deserve special attention.

In a very perceptive article, A.K. Ramanujan (1980) has drawn attention to the fact that the Indian thinking, far from being a unitary trend, is relativistic or context-dependent. He cites the case of his own father, who was without any friction in his mind and simultaneously a top-ranking scientist, mathematician and a pious Hindu performing various rituals and rites at home.

In his book *Gandhi's Political Philosophy: A Critical Examination*, Bhiku Parekh (1995: 85-109) lists the following as components of Gandhi's own identification of Sanatana Dharma or Indian identity: a) universe as one vast *yajna*; b) permeation of cosmic spirit in all creation; c) indivisibility of man; and d) viewing all human actions as grateful offerings at the cosmic altar.

In an essay entitled "The Comprehensive Indian Mind", Charles Moore (1967: 12-16) has listed as many as seventeen important principles of Indian thought. These include a spiritual bent of mind, belief in *Karma,* 'sense for the infinite', importance of intuition, synthetic conception of truth, deep concern with inner man, introspective approach to truth, and need for moral purification. Wilhelm Halbfass's book *Tradition and Reflection: Explorations in Indian Thought* examines some of these themes in a very detailed way (Halbfass 1991).

The Indian philosopher P.K. Mahapatra (2009) has argued that the early Orientalists (both European and Indian) looked at the Indian mind in a stereotyped fashion: "that the Indian mind is predominantly mystical, that the Indian tradition and culture is stagnant and endures for centuries without change, that the Indian attitude to values is spiritual, pessimistic and life-negating ..." (*Ibid.*: 14). He goes on to point out that a comprehensive study of the Indian philosophical systems such as the Charavaka and Vaisesika schools "well reveal its rich variety, not enblocked as mystical, spiritual, other-worldly and stagnant, but as practical, life-affirming, liberal and open to change." (*Ibid.:* 16).

In a very illuminating essay entitled "The 'Sanatani' Mahatma? Re-reading Gandhi, Post-Hindutva", Makarand Paranjape considers the Sanatana Parampara as a certain way of locating the self, the society and the cosmos. He spells out its principal features as follows: a) its lack of fixed point of beginning or closure; b) its pluralistic character; c) its lack of a central text or founder; d) its tendency to sacralize the world and all objects; and e) its non-exclusivity.

> The Sanatani is not anthropocentric, logocentric, or even theocentric, but radically self-centric, where self is, ultimately, non-separate, radically relational, and co-extensive with the cosmos. The Sanatani is not fixated on time, but on the untimely and timeless... The Sanatani also has a complex sense of causality called *Karma* and an equally complex sense of axiology called *Dharma* (Paranjape 2008: 207).

In his seven celebrated lectures delivered in Cambridge University in 1882 for the benefit of candidates selected for the

Fig. 5.1 Friedrich Max Müller (1823–1900), the celebrated German Indologist of the nineteenth century.

Indian Civil Service and published as a book entitled *India: What Can It Teach Us?*, Max Müller (2000) made a laudable attempt at correcting the negative picture of India and its heritage created in England by the publication of books like James Mill's *History of India* and Thomas Macaulay's scorn for Oriental learning. Emboldened by the fruits of German and French scholarship to unearth a "treasure house of ideas and systems of thought" from Sanskrit literature, Max Müller argued that it was possible to discover "the grains of solid gold in the dark mines of Eastern Philosophy". The famous passage 'I should point to India' is a truly measured assessment of India's contribution to human thought. He highlighted the human interest embodied in Sanskrit literature, the tenets of Vedic religion and the lofty principles of Vedanta (Fig. 5.1).

One may also consider what psychologists have to tell us about the character of the Indian mind. Here the observations of Sudhir Kakar are very useful. Kakar is a well-known psychoanalyst in the country and is acclaimed as one among 25 major thinkers of the world (Fig. 5.2). Arising from long experiences with his patients, his reading of the ancient Indian texts and his anthropological understanding of the Indian way of life, Kakar has arrived at his own perception of the Indianness or spirit of

Fig. 5.2 Sudhir Kakar (1938–), a noted psychoanalyst and writer.

India in two of his books entitled *The Inner World: Psychoanalytical Study of Childhood and Society in India* (Kakar 2008) and *The Indians: Portrait of a People* (Kakar and Kakar 2007). The Kakars quote approvingly Nehru's statement in his *The Discovery of India* that in India, with a long cultural background and a common outlook on life, there developed a spirit which is peculiar to it and which is impressed on all its people, irrespective of differences among themselves. They say further that this spirit of India is not something ethereal to be located in the realms of aesthetics, philosophy and religion but runs through even folk-tales, music and mundane matters like personal hygiene. This identity is not a fixed, unchanging entity but in fact profited from time to time from encounters with outside elements.

The Kakars (2007: 4) list the following four elements as the key building-blocks of the Indian identity: a) an ideology of family and other crucial human relationships derived from the institution of joint family; b) social relations which are basically governed by caste considerations; c) an understanding of the human body and its various processes, which is essentially based on Ayurveda; and d), most important from the point of view of this paper, a cultural imagination replete with many shared myths and legends drawn particularly from the two great epics *Ramayana* and

Mahabharata and which envisages a romantic vision of human life and context-dependent way of thinking. Certain core ideas derived from the Hindu world-view have permeated the Indian mind: a) *Moksha* or liberation through self-realization and belief in higher reality; b) *Dharma* or righteous conduct, which is context-dependent; and c) *Karma* principle, which emphasizes the role of meritorious actions that govern present and even future life (*Ibid*: 180-201).

Place of the Past

The Kakars hold the culturally shared part of the mind to be a key component of the spirit of India. What does it consist of? The Kakars (*Ibid*: 181) respond in these words:

> ...Here we are not concerned so much with philosophical doctrines that are relevant only for religious and intellectual elites but with the beliefs and attitudes—many of them not conscious—of a vast number of Indians that are reflected in their lives, their songs and their stories. These beliefs are disseminated through myths and legends, proverbs and metaphors, enacted in religious rituals, conveyed through tales told to children, given a modern veneer in Bollywood films and television serials, and glimpsed in the admonitions of parents or in the vision they have of their children's future. The world view that we are talking about, then, is absorbed from early on in life, and not through the head but the heart.

Using psychoanalytical perspectives, Kakar attempts to reconstruct the psycho-social background of Indianness or identity. Freud recognized long ago that cultural traditions are internalized during childhood in the individual's superego, which is built on "the model of the parents' superego: it takes over the same contents, it becomes the vehicle of tradition and of all the age-long values which have been handed over in this way from generation to generation" (Kakar 2008: 11). Then Kakar points out that the roots of culture in the psyche penetrate below the crusty layer of superego. Mediated through persons responsible for the infant's earliest care, cultural values are, from the beginning, an intimate and inextricable part of the ego. The ego develops in interdependence with the society into which the person is born. It is in particular the mother's responses and cares which shape the infant's new individuality and nurture his capacity, in socially approved ways, to transform passive experience into action. Continuing his analysis of the origins of cultural attitudes in the human individuals, Kakar writes (*Ibid*: 15):

> An exploration of the psychological terrain of the Indian world must begin with the cluster of ideas, historically derived, selected and refined, through which Hindu culture has traditionally structured the beliefs and behaviours of its members. At the heart of this cluster of governing ideas is a coherent, consistent world image in which the goal of human existence, the ways to reach this goal, the errors to be avoided and the obstacles to be expected along the way are all dramatically conveyed. I am not talking here of Hindu philosophy in the sense of abstract intellectualized concepts accessible only to an elite priesthood of interpreters, but of prescriptive configuration of ideal purposes, values and beliefs which percolate into the everyday life of ordinary people and give it form and meaning.

The import of the above citations from the works of various writers is that there does exist an Indianness or identity, which cuts across various regions and peoples in the country and that the Indian mind has provided a secure place for the past. In fact, the Indian psyche *sans* a sense of the past is unintelligible. To that extent, one may justifiably argue that the Indian psyche is past itself or else nothing. While making these claims, one does of course recognize the existence of dissenting voices and doubting Thomases. For instance, India has been called a wounded or decaying civilization with "no historical notion of the past, no identity beyond the tenuous ecumenism of Hindu beliefs" (Naipaul 1976: 184).

Manifestations and Sources of the Sense of Past

Now let us consider the next question: Where does this sense of the past manifest itself among the people, literate or non-literate? General writers and thinkers are one category of students of the pastness who take deep interest in history and other topics related to the country's heritage. Their motives are varied.

One may take, for instance, Pandit Nehru's *The Discovery of India*; it has been called "a great jumble of a book which bears the marks of haste and tension" and an example of "woolly writing" (Gopal 1976: 298). But the fact of the matter is that Nehru never claimed to be a historian and it was far from his desire to add another book to the library of books on Indian history (Fig. 5.3). He confesses that he did not posses the mood for knowledge of the past in the academic sense. Rather, he viewed history as a window for understanding the present. As he himself clarifies:

> I came late to history and, even then, not through the usual road of learning a mass of facts and dates and drawing conclusions and inferences from them, unrelated to my life's course. So long as I did this, history had little significance for me... some mixture of thought and emotion and urges, of which I was dimly aware, led me to action, and action, in its turn, sent me back to thought and a desire to understand the present. The roots of the present lay in the past and so I

Fig. 5.3 Pandit Jawaharlal Nehru (1889–1964), the first Prime Minister of India.

> made voyages of discovery into the past, ever seeking a clue in it, if any such existed, to the understanding of the present (Nehru 1960: 90).

Nehru also makes it abundantly clear that the country's past never made any sense to him unless it was made to touch on the present. In his own words:

> ...The past oppresses me or fills me sometimes with its warmth when it touches on the present, and becomes, as it were, an aspect of that living present. If it does not do so, then it is cold, barren, lifeless, uninteresting... (*Ibid*: 22).

Remarkable too is Nehru's grasp of history of the world as reflected in the letters he wrote to his daughter Indira from prison, which were later published as *Glimpses of World History* (Nehru 1962). He provides a fascinating account of the entire story of man from prehistoric to modern times through ancient and medieval epochs. A person with such a broad sweep of history is bound to be aware of the universalist dimensions of heritage. In an eloquent passage in *The Discovery of India*, he raises the questions of inheritance and identity and answers these himself:

> What is my inheritance? To what am I an heir? To all that humanity has achieved during tens of thousands of years, to all that it has thought and felt and suffered and taken pleasure in, to its cries of triumph, to that astonishing adventure of man which began so long ago and yet continues and beckons to us. To all this and more, in common with all men.... (Nehru 1960: 22-23).

Nehru's vision of history was greatly influenced by humanist philosophy (Gokhale 1978).

One can easily multiply examples of such non-specialist writings covering the whole range of Indology—religion, philosophy, history, culture, languages, etc. The writings of Vivekananda and Aurobindo on Indian religion and philosophy are well known. In western India, Barrister Vasudeva Kirtikar

(1924) wrote an excellent commentary on the Upanishads. Mahamahopadhyaya P.V. Kane's (1930) *History of the Dharmasastras* and D.D. Kosambi's (1965) *The Culture and Civilization of Ancient India in Historical Outline* are other noteworthy examples. Many examples of such writings could be cited from other parts of the country. A robust sense of the past was both the cause and the consequence of these writings.

But interest in the past is surely not limited to the circle of intellectuals. It finds expression among both educated laymen and non-literate groups spread across the length and breadth of the whole country. While they may not evince much interest in the latest trends in microphysics or molecular biology, they do display a sense of the past in everyday life. Recounting his experiences in this regard, arising from extensive journeys all across the county, Nehru (1960: 55) enthusiastically writes:

> ...Everywhere I found a cultural background which had exerted a powerful influence on their lives. This background was a mixture of popular philosophy, tradition, history, myth and legend, and it was not possible to draw a line between any of these. Even the entirely uneducated and illiterate shared this background. The old epics of India, the *Ramayana* and the *Mahabharata* and other books, in popular translations and paraphrases, were widely known among the masses, and every incident and story and moral in them was engraved on the popular mind and gave a richness and content to it. Illiterate villagers would know hundreds of verses by heart and their conversation would be full of references to them or to some story with a moral, enshrined in some old classic. Often I was surprised by some such literary turn given by a group of villages to a simple talk about present-day affairs. If my mind was full of pictures from recorded history and more-or-less ascertained fact, I

realized that even the illiterate peasant had a picture gallery in his mind, though this was largely drawn from myth and tradition and epic heroes and heroines, and only very little from history. Nevertheless, it was vivid enough.

I would like to cite some instances to illustrate how deeply the Indian mind is infused with values or life-guiding principles derived from the past:

1. "Protect Dharma and you will be protected by Dharma!"—Exhortation in Telugu inscribed on a truck forming part of public transport system.
2. *Lakshman rekha*—subtitle of a commercial product called Crazy Lines for keeping away cockroaches from cooked food items.
3. "Observance of *Lakshman rekha* is as important in international affairs as in personal life"—Former Prime Minister P.V. Narasimha Rao in his Address to the joint session of the U.S. Congress.
4. "You are truly personification of Sita"—An elderly gentleman's statement after he unexpectedly prostrated himself at a social gathering in New Delhi before Deepika Chikalia who played the role of Sita in the popular T.V. serial on the *Ramayana*.
5. "Please don't play the role of Narada Muni"—Congress spokesman Dr. Abhishek Singhvi's request to the T.V. anchor Arnab Goswami who was trying to pit him against the B.J.P. spokesman on the show.
6. "Mahabharat in the Ambani family"—Newspaper headline highlighting the fratricidal business feud between Mukesh Ambani and his brother Anil Ambani.
7. "What I know is like the size of a rice grain and what I don't know is the size of a mountain"—Prof. H.D.

Sankalia's answer quoting Sant Tukaram's words to a query in an interview on the All India Radio about his academic achievements.

8. "Ram, Ram… Ram, Ram"—Mode of greeting each other common among the peasant folk of the Deccan.

Such instances are commonplace in daily life in India. A variety of metaphors, similies, narration of anecdotes, tales, allegories, aphorisms, exhortations, warnings, proverbs, etc. taken from the past mediate the day-to-day transactions in life.

The following are the major sources from which the people derive their understanding of the past:

a) The *Rig Veda* and other Vedic texts including the Upanishads.
b) The stories from the epics *Mahabharata* and *Ramayana* comprising original Sanskrit texts and numerous regional versions which localize the events and places, thereby bringing the themes and personalities closer to the hearts of people (see Richman 1992; Thapar 2002: 647-79, 1055-78).
c) Dos and Don'ts prescribed in the *Bhagavadgita.*
d) The Puranas and other religious as well as secular texts of the historical period.
e) The Buddhist and Jaina texts.
f) Sant literature of the early or late mediaeval periods in various regional languages.
g) Episodes from the lives of famous personalities of the medieval period (e.g., Deshpande 2007; Shail Mayaram 2008).

Ideas or metaphors drawn from these various secular and religious sources are effectively reached even to the non-literate groups by adopting a variety of techniques and methods of folk communication. The more important among these methods of popular education are as under:

a) Tales, myths and stories narrated at home to children by parents and other elders.
b) Late evening performances (dramas, plays, dance-dramas, shadow-plays, *Harikirtans*, *Yakshaganas*, *burra-kathas*, *powadas*, etc.), which used to enthral village audiences.[1] To a great extent these folk media have now been taken over by T.V. and radio serials.
c) Recitations on various religious and secular occasions, such as marriages, house-warming, and temple ceremonies, including almanac-reading by the village priest on the New Year eve.
d) Short- or long-distance pilgrimages to religious centres which, as pointed out by Radha Kumud Mookerji (1954) and other writers, reinforce the geographical and cultural unity of India.

Commenting on the effect which these oral and visual presentations of themes taken from the past have on the minds of the people, Max Müller (2000: 74-75) writes:

> ...we are told that the ancient epic poems of the Mahabharata and Ramayana are still recited in the temples for the benefit of visitors, and that in the villages large crowds assemble around *Kathaka*, the reader of these ancient Sanskrit poems, often interrupting his recitations with tears and sighs, when the hero of the poem is sent into banishment, while when he returns to his kingdom, the houses of the village are adorned with lamps and garlands...

It is little surprise then that the past has become an inseparable part of the Indian ethos. It is in this respect that the

Indian mind differs from the American, African or Australian mind. Across the ages, this component of pastness has moulded the Indian character. It is again this component which supplied strength to Indian society in facing powerful political and religious influences from outside. This is the reason why the stories from the epics and Puranas and the writings of medieval saints continue to exercise undiminished influence on the minds of Indian people.

DISCUSSION

Unfortunately, attempts at analyzing these long and widespread non-professional renderings of the country's past and their use in everyday life are few and far between. In his recent book entitled *The Ways of Understanding the Past*, D.P. Chattopadhyaya (2001: 22-60) has argued that, while Homer's works *Iliad* and *Odyssey* have practically disappeared from the Greek life, the epics *Mahabharata* and *Ramayana* are still a living force in the Indian context. The original Sanskrit texts and their numerous regional editions are for the Indian people rich sources of a form of history called *Itihasa*, which is different from scientific conception of history guided by spatio-temporal and causal parameters. The *aitihasik* (adverbial form of *Itihasa*) mode of expression of the past has its own distinctive character. Quoting Aurobindo, Chattopadhyaya (2001: 55) says that the two epics express the mind of the nation:

> ...In *itihasa* legendary tradition is creatively blended with symbolic myths and tales with a view to conveying some spiritual and social message to the people at large. In the literary epics... one finds not only *Dharmakanda* but also *Karmakanda* of human life. In these works, aesthetics, emotion, poetry, fiction and romance are imaginatively

> mingled with philosophy, ethics and social and political ideas. Though the epics are dominated by the narrative consideration of the main stories, the underlying ethico-religious (*dharma*) tone is unmistakable. Personal and political struggles are given the form of the struggle between the godheads of truth and light, on the one hand, and the forces of darkness, division and falsehood, on the other....

We may recall here that long ago V.S. Sukhtankar (1957) drew attention to the mundane, ethical and metaphysical meanings of the *Mahabharata* (see also various essays in Prasad 2009).

In a thought-provoking and hard-hitting essay entitled "History's Forgotten Doubles", presented as the Opening Address at the World History Conference held at the Wesleyan University, U.S.A., in 1994, the noted psychoanalyst and thinker Ashis Nandy stoutly defended the Indians' construction of their past and its use (Fig. 5.4; see also Deftereos 2013). He says that this construction of the past is not alternate history but is actually ahistorical and as such constitutes an alternative *to* (*sic*) history. It is history's doubles. In an eloquent statement, he articulates his point of view in these words:

Fig. 5.4 Ashis Nandy (1937–), a well-known social scientist from Delhi.

> However odd this might sound to contemporary historians, millions of people still live outside history. They *do* (*sic*) have

> theories of the past; they do believe that the past is important and shapes the present and the future, but they also recognize, confront and live with a past different from the one constructed by historians and historical consciousness. They even have a different way of arriving at the past (Nandy 2002: 83).

Nandy identifies two important characteristics of this ahistorical construction of the past. First, in this tradition it is mostly through myths that experiences of the past are organized. The organization of these experiences involves the principle of what Nandy calls principled forgetfulness.

> All myths are morality tales. Mythologization is also moralization; it involves a refusal to separate the remembered past from its ethical meaning in the present. For this refusal, it is often important *not* (*sic*) to remember the past, objectively, clearly, or in its entirety (*Ibid*: 86).

Secondly, unlike the historians who are narcissistic about their norms of historiography and thereby suffer from the Freudian fantasy of immortality, the ahistorical tradition, in order to render historical consciousness more humane and less impersonal, adopts elastic guidelines while scanning the sources. As an example of this ahistorical tradition, Nandy cites the psychoanalyst Girindrasekhar Bose's study of the Puranas and epics undertaken in the 30s of the last century (Nandy 1998: 119-31).

Nandy does not hesitate to chide the country's historians for their lack of self-reflexivity and for their unwillingness to produce "radial criticism of history from within the ranks of historians". He indicts that the 'rightist' and 'leftist' groups of historians for their total lack of understanding of people's perception of their past and for advocating their own points of view about the 'historical truths' in the case of Ayodhya temple–mosque controversy. Nandy (2002: 108-9) concludes his Address in unambiguous words:

> ...The domination of that consciousness (concept of objective history derived from the West) has now become, as the confrontation at Ayodhya shows, a cultural and political liability. In a civilization where there are many bitter memories and animosities, to absolutize them with the help of the European concept of history is to attack the organizing principles of the civilization. Particularly so, given that South Asian historians, though otherwise a garrulous lot, have produced no radical critique of history, perhaps not even an authentic history of history. They have sought to historicize everything, but never the idea of history itself. For, historicizing the idea of history is to historicize the historians themselves. As I have said, such self-confrontation has not been the strong suit of historians; there are very poor checks in history against the violence and cruelty that may follow from uncritical acceptance of the idea of history.

The critical observations made by Nandy are being cited here not to diminish the importance of history, archaeology and other disciplines forming part of heritage studies. Far from being fit cases for closure, these disciplines have before them much unexplored raw data to deal with and, for attending to this job in a meaningful way, they also need to constantly revise their aims and methods. At the same time, they need to descend from their ivory-towers and devote some time for considering the whats, hows and whys of people's constructions of the past in the country. It is easy to brand these versions of the past as populist and relegate them to the background. For example, the *Ramayana* and

Mahabharata serials on the television have been called creations meant for catering to the fantasies of the Indian mind. William Dalrymple's book *The Last Mughal* published in 2006 has been dubbed as a piece of journalistic writing and Gandhism depicted in the Hindi film *Lage Raho Munnabhai* has been called a farce of history. There is some truth in all these comments but this does not obviate the need for a systematic sociological and psychological analysis of the nature, methods and uses of the popular conceptions of the past discussed above. In other words, the issue is one of investigating whether the sense of past that existed in ancient India, as argued convincingly by Pathak (1966), Sharma (2003), Thapar (2002: 123-72; 2013) and other writers, is still a living tradition among the people. The aims, methods and targeted audiences of the scientific or truth-centered conception of the past which the historians and archaeologists employ and the ethics-oriented popular conceptions are admittedly different but these are not necessarily antithetical. These may actually be mutually complementary. While the scientific constructions of the past can render the popular versions less fantasy-ridden, more objective and hence less amenable to fundamentalist use by vested interests, the popular conceptions could bring in a larger sense of humanism and purpose in truth-finding and objectivity-centred reconstructions of the historians.

It is my understanding that there are not one but two swords of Damocles hanging over heritage studies in India. First, the processes of modernization and globalization unleashed in the country in recent times are not only swiftly obliterating the soft and hard components of the heritage but are also tending to make people lose their moorings in the past. Secondly, the number of groups misusing the past for furthering their own vested politico-religious and communal interests is on the rise. In order to cope up with situations like these, it is important to introduce the past as part of liberal education at school, college and higher levels. The hymn about unknown beginnings and ends, as cited in the Nasadiya Sukta of the *Rig Veda*, the Upanishadic concept of Brahman as the ultimate reality, the Indian conception of the scientific method, the concept of Dharma and others enshrined in the two epics, and the Buddhist concept of *Paticca Samuppada* are just only some among a whole assortment of concepts that could form part of this scheme of liberal education. In fact, ideas and concepts encompassing sociopolitical, philosophical and religious thought of the land as well as arts, literature and scientific achievements of ancient and medieval periods all could form part of a full-fledged course on Indian thought at both under- and post-graduate levels. To my knowledge, no such integrated course on Indian thought is available at the Indian universities (Paddayya 2000b).

It may sound strange but the fact remains that some of the colonial administrators linked the future of India with instruction in its ancient learning. For instance, it was this notion which Mountstuart Elphinstone, the enlightened Governor of Bombay Presidency, had in his mind when he established in 1821 the Hindu College in Pune, the core institution of the present Deccan College. While addressing the Directors of the East India Company, who had objected to the establishment of this college, Elphinstone wrote:

> We cannot but think that the future attainments of the natives will be increased in extent as well as in variety by being as it were engrafted on their own previous knowledge and imbued with their own original and peculiar character (as quoted in Paddayya 2002: 60).

More recently, Bruce Rich, a Senior Attorney and head of an environmental organization in the U.S., has published a full book in which he fervently argues that Kautilya and Ashoka have much relevance in the contemporary world. As he puts it:

> ...What I hoped to do is to examine them as archetypes, metaphors and sources of inspiration for thinking about the perennial conundrums of politics, economics and ethics, which today are played out on a global scale as never before... my hope has been to offer a personal contribution to showing the relevance of a part of ancient Indian thought and history to the challenges of the 21st century (Rich 2008: XV).

In this connection, it is interesting to note that the Indian society's age-old traditions of austerity and frugality have imparted but only limited success to the new consumer culture of shopping malls, credit cards and global brands (Mathur 2010).

The benefits of this liberal education highlighting the central importance of concepts embodying our past should also be reached to the common man. His ability to separate fact from fantasy should not be underestimated. As one enters the threshold of adulthood and begins to experience the doings of man and happenings in nature in a direct way, even persons without 'read and write' literacy begin to realize that behind all the divinities they worship and the sundry rituals and rites they follow in day-to-day life, there are some underlying principles and concepts. Max Müller cites an example. He remarks that the discovery of the Brahman or Paramatman no doubt requires observance of moral and intellectual disciplines but immediately points out that

> ... those who had not yet discovered it, were allowed to worship lower gods, and to employ more poetical names to

> satisfy their human wants. Those who knew the other gods to be but names or persons—personae or masks, in the true sense of the word *pratikas*, as they call them in Sanskrit—knew also that those who worshipped these names or persons, worshipped in truth the Highest Self, though ignorantly.... (Max Müller 2000: 224).

Liberal education about the past could sharpen common man's understanding of the conceptual background of myths, legends and figures permeating the past.

It is amazing that Sir William Jones recognized the larger social purpose of education more than two years ago. In a famous oration delivered at the University of Oxford in 1773, he remarked thus:

> ...let us not so far deceive ourselves, as to imagine, that Learning without Virtue has any merit, though Virtue without Learning may justly claim the highest encomium: let us remember that the sole purpose and tendency of human knowledge is to make us serviceable to our friends, our country and all mankind; that speculation is only commendable, as far as it may supply us with Wisdom and Valour in active life, and that all arts, literature, science, cease to be laudable, as soon as they cease to be beneficial (Jones 1807: 13).

These suggested measures to educate the mind of common man fit in well with Amartya Sen's (1999) notion of development as freedom, where development is viewed as an agent-centred process in which individuals can take ideas from the community's pool of values and concepts and contribute to the formulation of public policy. Sen (1996) considers the country's past as an important source of ideas and believes that people do benefit from it. We shall conclude by citing a recent instance of the soundness of common man's judgement. Against the background of Angst generated among the intellectuals in the West (the Indian T.V. channels and print media too) that the "uneducated, poor and decidedly unmodern masses" in India might vote to power a hotch-potch coalition government in the 2009 general elections, Sen argued—clearly many days before the announcement of results—at a panel discussion in the Royal Society of Arts in London that India is a land of *civilizational continuity* (emphasis added) and that the Indians' sense of the past and their plasticity, flexibility and adaptability would not allow democracy to collapse (Datta-Ray 2009). Surely the common man and his sense of the past did not disappoint us!

The purpose of this lecture is to induce younger workers to adopt methodological and theoretical approaches from social psychology and take up regular research projects for understanding in a more systematic way people's perceptions of the past and the uses they put them to.[2]

NOTES

1. The role played by *Harikirtan* has been commented upon by several workers, e.g. 1) Kunal Chakrabarti, "Kirtan and Social Organization in Mediaeval Bengal", *Indian Economic and Social History Review,* Vol. 28, 1991, pp. 445-61, review essay on H.R. Sanyal's book *Bangla Kirtaner Itihasa,* Calcutta, 1989; 2) Y.B. Damle, "A Note on Harikatha", *Bulletin of the Deccan College Research Institute,* Vol. 17, 1955, pp. 15-19. *Kathayatra,* involving a series of week-long story-telling stage performances, was held in Pune in December 2012. Girish Karnad and other actors and writers emphasized the traditional role played by these folk performances in the inculcation of values in society.

2. This is the theme of the Dr. C. Meenakshi memorial lecture delivered by me at the Bhandarkar Research Institute, Pune, in June 2009. It was later published as a research paper entitled "The Place of the Past in the Indian Mind" in the *Journal of the Asiatic Society* (Kolkata), Volume 53, No.1, 2011, pp. 1-18. I have made slight changes in the present text. I am grateful to the Honorary Secretary of the Society for permission to reprint the paper under the present title.

REFERENCES

Chakrabarti, D.K. 1997. *Colonial Indology: Socio-Politics of the Ancient Indian Past.* New Delhi: Munshiram Manoharlal Publishers.

——. 2009. *The Battle for Ancient India: An Essay in the Socio-Politics of Indian Archaeology.* New Delhi: Aryan Books International.

Chattopadhyaya, D.P. 2001. *The Ways of Understanding the Past: Mythic, Epic, Scientific and Historical.* New Delhi: Centre for Studies in Civilizations.

Datta-Ray, Deep K. 2009. Tradition and Modernity: India's Past Informs India's Political Present. *The Times of India,* dated 14th May 2009.

Deshpande, Prachi. 2007.*Creative Pasts: Historical Memory and Identity in Western India, 1700-88.* Delhi: Permanent Black.

Deftereos, Christine. 2013. *Ashis Nandy and the Cultural Politics of Selfhood.* New Delhi: Sage Publications.

Gokhale, B.G. 1978. Nehru and History. *History and Theory* 17: 311-22.

Gopal, S. 1976. *Jawaharlal Nehru: A Biography* (Volume 1, 1888-1947). New Delhi: Oxford University Press.

Halbfass, Wilhelm. 1991. *Tradition and Reflection: Explorations in Indian Thought.* Albany: University of New York Press.

Inden, R. 1990. *Imagining India.* Oxford: Basil Blackwell.

Illich, Ivan. 2002. Mnemosyne: The Mold of Memory. In Ivan Illich, *The Mirror of the Past: Lectures and Addresses 1978-1990.* New York. As quoted by Ashis Nandy in *The Romance of the State and the Fate of Dissent in the Tropics,* 2002, pp. 102. New Delhi: Oxford University Press.

Ingalls, D.H.H. 1960. On the Study of the Past. *Journal of the American Oriental Society* 80: 191-97.

Jones, William. 1807. *The Collected Works of Sir William Jones,* Volume 1 (edited by Lord Teignmouth). London: John Stockdale and John Walter. Reprinted in 1993 by Curzon Press, London, with an Introduction by Garland Cannon.

Kakar, Sudhir. 2008. *The Inner World: A Psychoanalytical Study of Childhood and Society in India.* New Delhi: Oxford University Press. Originally published in 1978.

Kakar, Sudhir and Katharina Kakar. 2007. *Indians: Portrait of a People.* New Delhi: Penguin Books.

Kane, P.V. 1930-1962. *History of the Dharmasastras (Ancient and Medieval Religious and Civil Law)*, Volumes I to V. Pune: Bhandarkar Oriental Research Institute.

Kirtikar, Vasudeva J. 1924. *Studies in the Vedanta.* Mumbai: D.B. Taraporevala and Sons.

Kosambi, D.D. 1965. *The Culture and Civilization of Ancient India in Historical Outline.* London: Routledge.

Mahapatra, P.K. 2009. Survey of Modern Writings on Classical Indian Ethics: Methodological Hints for Appraising Ethics. In Rajendra Prasad (ed.), *A Historical-Developmental Study of Classical Indian Philosophy of Morals,* pp. 13-45. New Delhi: Centre for Studies in Civilizations.

Mathur, Nita. 2010. Shopping Malls, Credit Cards and Global Brands: Consumer Culture and Lifestyle of India's New Middle Class. *South Asia Research* 30(3): 211-31.

Max Müller, F. 2000. *India: What Can It Teach Us?* New Delhi: Penguin Books. Originally published in 1882.

Mookerji, Radha Kumud. 1954. *Fundamental Unity of India.* Mumbai: Bharatiya Vidya Bhavan.

Moore, Charles A. 1967. Introduction: The Comprehensive Indian Mind. In Charles A. Moore (ed.), *The Indian Mind: Essentials of Indian Philosophy and Culture,* pp. 12-16. Honolulu: University of Hawaii Press.

Naipaul, V.S. 1976. *India: A Wounded Civilization.* New York: Vintage Books.

Nandy, Ashis. 1998. *Return from the Exile.* New Delhi: Oxford University Press.

——. 2002. History's Forgotten Doubles. In Ashis Nandy, *Romance of the State and the Fate of Dissent in the Tropics,* pp. 83-109. Originally published in *History and Theory* 34, 1985, pp. 44-66.

Nehru, Jawaharlal. 1960. *The Discovery of India.* London: Meridian Books.

——. 1962. *Glimpses of World History.* Mumbai: Asia Publishing House. Originally published in 1934-35.

Paddayya, K. 2002a. A Review of Theoretical Perspectives in Indian Archaeology. In S. Settar and R. Korisettar (eds.), *Indian Archaeology in Retrospect—Archaeology and Historiography: History, Theory and Method,* Volume IV, pp. 117-57. New Delhi: ICHR and Manohar.

——. 2002b. On Some Aspects of the Early History of the Deccan College, Pune. *Bulletin of the Deccan College Research Institute* 60-61 (2000-01): 29-64.

——. 2002c. Ancient Indian Thought: A Component of Liberal Education. *University News* (31 December 2001-6 January 2002): 3-9.

Paranjape, Makarand. 2007. The 'Sanatani' Mahatma? Re-reading Gandhi Post-Hindutva. In Allen Douglas (ed.), *The Philosophy of Mahatma Gandhi for the Twenty-first Century,* pp. 201-14. New Delhi: Oxford University Press.

Parekh, Bhikhu. 1995. *Gandhi's Political Philosophy: A Critical Examination.* Delhi: Ajanta Books International.

Pathak, V.S. 1966. *Ancient Historians of India: A Study in Historical Biographies.* Mumbai: Asia Publishing House.

Prasad, Rajendra (ed.). 2009. *A Historical and Developmental Study of Classical Indian Philosophy of Morals.* New Delhi: Centre for Studies in Civilizations.

Ramanujan, A.K. 1980. Is There an Indian Way of Thinking? An Informal Essay. In Mckim Marriott (ed.), *India through the Ages,* pp. 41-58. New Delhi: Oxford University Press.

Rich, Bruce. 2008. *To Uphold the World: The Message of Ashoka and Kautilya for the 21st Century.* New Delhi: Penguin Books.

Richman, Paula (ed.). 1992. *Many Ramayanas: The Diversity of a Narrative Tradition.* New Delhi: Oxford University Press.

Said, Edward. 1978.*Orientalism.* New York: Pantheon Books.

Sen, Amartya. 1996. *On Interpreting India's Past.* Kolkata: The Asiatic Society.

——. 1999. Capability and Well-being. In M.C. Nussbaum and Amartya Sen (eds.), *The Quality of Life,* pp. 30-53. New Delhi: Oxford University Press.

Sharma, Arvind. 2003. *Hinduism and its Sense of History.* New Delhi: Oxford University Press.

Sukthankar, V.S. 1957. *On the Meaning of the Mahabharata.* Mumbai: The Asiatic Society.

Thapar, Romila. 1968. Interpretations of Ancient Indian History. *History and Theory* 7(3): 318-35.

——. 2002. *Cultural Pasts: Essays in Early Indian History.* New Delhi: Oxford University Press.

——. 2013. *The Past Before Us: Historical Traditions of Early North India.* Ranikhet: Permanent Black.

Van der Veer, P. 1999. Monumental Texts. In Daud Ali (ed.), *Invoking the Past: The Uses of History in South Asia,* pp. 133-45. Delhi: Oxford University Press.

CHAPTER VI

The Relevance of the Past
From Sir William Jones to Amartya Sen

There is a long-standing debate in the social sciences about their aims and goals. The aims of historical sciences as regular branches of knowledge have changed from time to time over the last two hundred years. Simple and innate human urges like respect for ancestors, curiosity about antiquarian remains of the surrounding area and appreciation of their aesthetic properties, while still being valid and proper, eventually gave way to regular knowledge-seeking interests (for analysis of benefits and burdens of the past, see Lowenthal 1985). In archaeology, the Three-Age System proposed by C.J. Thomsen in the early part of the 19th century was the first major step in this direction. It initiated the goal of framing culture history. Later in the century, archaeology was introduced as a separate subject of study in some of the universities in Europe. Also, the detailed stratigraphical record exposed in the caves and open-air sites of western Europe and large-scale or horizontal excavations at the Bronze Age town sites in West Asia and the Mediterranean zone brought into relief the new knowledge-seeking goal of reconstruction of lifeways.

This topic of aims acquired a much sharper focus with the emergence of the New Archaeology in the 1960s; culture process became the focus of attention. In the 1980s, yet another upheaval took place in archaeology; ideational trends arguing for an archaeology of mind shot into prominence. All these developments basically concerned epistemological aspects and transformed archaeology into an active academic discipline (for details, see Paddayya 1990).

I propose to comment in this chapter on an aspect of the study of the past which has been skirted by the above-mentioned developments. This is the topic of its relevance to society at large. I am aware that historical realism has been a dominant trend in history since the time of Ranke. This trend insisted on knowing "what actually happened" and "seeing things as they really were." Another fallout of this trend is the insistence on studying the past for its own sake (Lemon 2003: 331-3; see also Southgate 1996: Chapters 2 and 3 and 2000: Chapter 1). Archaeologists, too, by and large still live in their own 'ivory-towers' and do not seem to take notice of the public dimensions of the study of the past. In his book *Archaeology Matters*, Jeremy Sabloff (2008) has drawn attention to the importance of the findings of action or applied archaeology to local communities. He asserts that action archaeology projects show that "archaeological research can be integral to efforts to improve the sustainability of our planet and the quality of life for people around the world ... (Sabloff 2008: 27).

In another publication, Smith (2009) reviewed the connecting appeal of past occurrences as such with another type of meaningfulness—ethical, political, religious, metaphysical, scientific or aesthetic. I wish to explore this theme of meaningfulness by taking up the ideas expressed by some professional as well as non-professional writers and identify, if possible, some common threads of thought among them. Finally,

Fig. 6.1 Sir William Jones (1746–1794), Founder-President of The Asiatic Society, Kolkata.

I shall argue that the study of the past should be made an important component of liberal education. The debate about the relevance of the past gains importance in India in the context of the ongoing processes of modernization and politico-religious discourses seriously affecting the fabric of the society and the worldview of the people.

Let us begin with the ideas of Sir William Jones himself (Fig. 6.1). It is well known that within a few years after his arrival in India he achieved enough proficiency in Sanskrit to be able to start reading the original texts and realize the wealth of knowledge contained in these writings. While he devoted his Annual Discourses to The Asiatic Society to make a comparative study of the Oriental languages, literatures, religions, philosophies, etc., he wrote articles on a variety of Indological topics ranging from ancient Indian chronology, religion, zodiac and music to mohua liquor-making and cure for snake-bite. It is also important to note that he was not cut off from the reality of social life in Asia. He stoutly opposed child labour and slavery and argued for equality of punishment to the Europeans and Indians. In order to augment food supplies, he even suggested that the large pandanus fruit should be adopted from the Andaman Islands.

More importantly, Sir William held that the highest goal of learning was the promotion of human happiness rather than the acquisition of pure knowledge. He gave explicit expression to this view at two places. In a short piece entitled 'Plan of an essay on education' written in his 23rd year (1769), Sir William viewed knowledge acquisition as only a secondary aim of education and asserted that its primary aim lay in the promotion of "good of ourselves and of our fellow creatures" (Jones 1807:155).

Sir William advocated this viewpoint in a more forceful way in his famous oration delivered at the University of Oxford on 9th July 1773. In his own inimitable words:

> ...let us not so far deceive ourselves, as to imagine, that Learning without Virtue has any merit, Virtue without Learning may justly claim the highest encomium: let us remember, that the sole purpose and tendency of human knowledge is to make us serviceable to our friends, our country and all mankind; that speculation is only commendable, as far as it may supply us with Wisdom and Valour in active life, and that all arts, literature, science, cease to be laudable, as soon as they cease to be beneficial (Jones 1807:12-13).

In fact, Jones was a universalist and wanted his knowledge of the Oriental lands to serve as a bridge for promoting understanding and universalist spirit among nations of the world.

We next come to C.J. Thomsen, the 19th century Curator of the Royal Danish Museum, who made a systematic study of the variegated collections that had accumulated there and recognized that the pre-Christian past of the area passed through three consecutive stages and called them the Stone, Bronze and Iron Ages. Thomsen thus introduced the element of logos or knowledge about the past into the study of antiquarian remains. No less important, he organized a three-phase display of objects and threw

Fig. 6.2 Sir William Matthews Flinders Petrie (1853–1942), the famous British Egyptologist.

open the museum gallery to the public. He took pleasure in taking the visitors round the galleries, particularly the country folk, as he believed that they would have useful information about similar objects from their own areas, with whose help he would be able to interpret in a better way the meanings of objects in his collections (Paddayya 1993).

Flinders Petrie was a famous Egyptologist of British origin who excavated pyramids for ten years from 1883 to 1892 (Fig. 6.2). Based upon his field experiences in Egypt, he wrote in 1904 what may well be the first book on method and theory in archaeology, entitled *Methods and Aims in Archaeology*. It is remarkable that a century ago, Petrie made two amazing observations which are now an accepted part of archaeological discourse. First, he anticipated the modern processual and ideational trends when he stated that archaeology is "the science which enquires into all the products and works of our own species, which shows what man has been doing in all ages and under all conditions, which reveal man's mind, his thoughts, his tastes and his feelings" (Petrie 1972:vii). Secondly, and more pertinently from the point of view of the present chapter, Petrie already recognized that archaeology provides more truly liberal education than any other subject. He writes:

> Archaeology—the knowledge of how man has acquired his present position and powers—is one of the widest studies ... it is best fitted to open the mind and to produce that type of wide interests and toleration which is the highest result of education (Petrie 1972: viii).

Thirty-five years later Grahame Clark, the famous Cambridge archaeologist, put forward similar ideas in a more elaborate way in his book *Archaeology and Society* which, although published in 1939, is "obstinately still alive." In the chapter entitled 'Prehistory and Today', Clark (1965:251-64) mentioned that archaeology, because it deals with visible remains, is a good source of leisure-filling and entertainment to both literate and non-literate persons. Clark further said that archaeology could also be a good medium of education because it helps people develop a sense of historical imagination and stimulates interest in geography by demonstrating how adjustments are made across the globe between people, habitats and biomes, and also because it promotes in human mind a strong sense of aesthetic appreciation. Secondly, Clark argued strongly in favour of the view that study of the past promotes social solidarity and integration by highlighting common traditions and common histories. In preliterate societies, consciousness of shared past is kept alive by myths and rituals and by stories relating to common ancestors.

H.D. Sankalia, an Indian contemporary of Professor Grahame Clark, advocated closely similar views about the relevance of archaeology (Figs. 6.3 and 6.4). In a short paper entitled 'Archaeology and Education' published in 1965, he argued that archaeology is a fit topic for inclusion in the school curriculum because it promotes among children a spirit of curiosity and adventure and also because it enhances a child's perception and understanding of the empirical world (Sankalia 1965). No less important, Sankalia visualized even a bigger role for the discipline: it paves the way for international goodwill and understanding

Fig. 6.3 Hasmukh Dhirajlal Sankalia (1908–1989) with school children in Pune city.

among the world's peoples by underscoring their common cultural roots.

Now let us consider briefly the views of two non-professional writers who chose to write on Indian history. It is well known that Nehru wrote the text of his famous book *The Discovery of*

Fig. 6.4 Hasmukh Dhirajlal Sankalia taking round visitors at the Tripuri excavation (Madhya Pradesh) in 1967.

India in five months in 1944 during his imprisonment in the Ahmadnagar jail. It was far from his desire to produce yet another addition to the existing list of books on Indian history. He confesses that he did not possess the mood for knowledge of the past in the academic sense. Rather, he viewed history as a window for understanding the present (for details about Nehru's concept of history, see Gokhale 1978). As he himself writes:

> I came late to history and, even then, not through the usual road of learning a mass of facts and dates and drawing conclusions and inferences from them, unrelated to my life's course. So long as I did this, history had little significance for me... some mixture of thought and emotion and urges, of which I was dimly aware, led me to action, and action, in its turn, sent me back to thought and a desire to understand the present. The roots of the present lay in the past and so I made voyages of discovery into the past, ever seeking a clue in it, if any such existed, to the understanding of the present.... (1960:9).

Nehru also makes it explicitly clear that the country's past never made any sense to him unless it was made to touch on the present. He expresses this feeling in explicit terms as follows:

> ...The past oppresses me or fills me sometimes with its warmth when it touches on the present, and becomes, as it were, an aspect of that living present. If it does not do so, then it is cold, barren, lifeless, uninteresting... (Nehru 1960: 22).

He continues further and says that writing history is a process similar to that of psychoanalysis, as applied to a race or to humanity, and brings some relief from the weight and burden of the past.

But Nehru, while considering individual trees, does not lose sight of the woods. He is fully aware of the universalist dimensions of the heritage. In a beautiful passage he raises the questions of inheritance and identity and answers it himself:

> What is my inheritance? To what am I an heir? To all that humanity has achieved during tens of thousands of years, to all that it has thought and felt and suffered and taken pleasure in, to its cries of triumph and its bitter agony of defeat, to that astonishing adventure of man which began so long ago and yet continues and beckons to us. To all this and more, in common with all men ... (1960:22-3).

We now take up the views of another noted non-professional writer on history. It is well known that Amartya Sen, regarded as the Buddha of welfare economics, gave a new definition of development (Fig. 6.5). In Sen's view, development is much more than causing improvements in the material conditions of existence. Sen contends that economic growth is not an end in itself but only a means towards the development of human individuals; and that the basic building-blocks of development are formed by the freedoms of individuals, (Sen 1999a). Sen developed the concept of development as freedom, where development is seen as an agent-centered process and where individuals are not treated as passive beneficiaries but rather as agents who can effectively shape their own destiny.

Fig. 6.5 Amartya Sen (1933–), Nobel Laureate in Economics.

Hence, there is a need to improve the freedoms/capabilities of individuals. Sen visualizes a reciprocal relationship between public policy and freedoms of individuals (Sen 1999b).

While exercising their freedoms, people take ideas from a general pool or matrix of social values or mores, of which historical consciousness or sense of the past is an important one. In three of his writings, Sen shows his awareness of the main lineaments of the subcontinent's past and emphasizes that the past is an important ingredient in forming the self-identity of a group or society (Sen 1993, 1996a, 1996b). In his own words:

> Our identities are strongly influenced by the past. The self-perceptions that characterize a group are associated with, and to a great extent defined by, the shared memories and recollections of the past, and by the agreed priorities and implicit allegiances that draw on these evocations (Sen 1996a: 1).

Secondly, far from maintaining that it is always the past which impinges on the present, Sen readily agrees that our interpretation of the past may be coloured by the contemporary concerns.

> The interpretations of India's past cannot but be sensitive to the concerns of today. Our identities cannot be defined independently of our traditions and past, but this does not indicate a linear sequence whereby we interpret our past first and then arrive at our identity, equipped to face our contemporary issues. On the contrary, our reading of the past and understanding of the present are interdependent... While we cannot live without our past, we need not live within it either (Sen 1996a: 38).

Thirdly, deriving strength from the hindsight provided by history, Sen argues strongly in favour of sociocultural and political pluralism. Using his review of the films made by Satyajit Ray, Sen holds that a critical openness of mind has an important role to play in understanding and appreciating the variety in human culture at the local, regional, national and international levels (Sen 1996b).

What is the import of the above-mentioned citations from various writers? It is clear that, while much of the academic debate in the historical sciences has been concerned with making improvements in the epistemological or knowledge-seeking realm, some of the writers did draw attention to the larger issue of the close relevance of the past to society at large. In the case of ancient regions like India, where the mind of an average citizen is imbued with a deep sense of the past, its study cannot just be a matter of intellectual or romantic adventure. The matter is certainly not like saying with Edmund Hillary that "I climbed Mount Everest because it is there!" The study of the past has the greatest social relevance. The great historian R.G. Collingwood wrote that history provides self-knowledge to man (Collingwood 1961). In our own country Kalhana, the author of Kashmir chronicle entitled *Rajatarangini*, put this notion of self-knowledge very well when he said 800 years ago: "This saga which is properly made should be useful for (a) king as a stimulant or as a sedative, like a psychic, according to time and place" (as quoted Majumdar 1961:21).

In view of the increasing pace of the processes of globalization and modernization operating in the country and also the menacing trend of misuse of the past by vested interests for narrow political and religious purposes, it is necessary to strengthen the common man's sense of the past by educating him about the past. Here, promotion of the Nehruvian concept of scientific temper of mind (Singh 1986; Paddayya 2012) and Amartya Sen's concept of critical openness of mind assume a large measure of importance. How do we achieve this? I would like to repeat a plea I have made elsewhere for the introduction of ancient Indian thought as a component of liberal education (Paddayya 2002). Ideas and concepts encompassing sociopolitical, philosophical and religious thought, arts, literature and scientific achievements of ancient and medieval periods, all could form part of a course on Indian thought. The hymn about unknown beginnings and ends, as given in the Nasadiya Sukta of the *Rig Veda*, the Upanishadic concept of Brahman as the ultimate reality, the Indian conception of scientific method, the concepts of Dharma, Laxman-rekha and a host of others enshrined in the epics *Mahabharata* and *Ramayana*, the Buddhist concept of *Paticca Samuppada* and the Ashokan precepts of *Danda Samata* and *Vyavahara Samata* and respect for other religious faiths are only some among the numerous items that could be included under this scheme of liberal education.

REFERENCES

Clark, J.G.D. 1965. *Archaeology and Society*. London: Methuen & Co. Originally published in 1939.

Collingwood, R.G. 1961. *The Idea of History*. Oxford: Oxford University Press.

Gokhale, Balakrishna Govind. 1978. Nehru and History. *History and Theory* 17: 311-22.

Jones, William. 1807. *The Collected Works of Sir William Jones*, Volume 1 (Edited by Lord Teignmouth). London: John Stockdale and John Walter. Reprinted in 1993 by Curzon Press, London, with an Introduction by Garland Cannon.

Lemon, M.C. 2003. *Philosophy of History: A Guide for Students.* London: Routledge.

Lowenthal, D. 1985. *The Past is a Foreign Country.* Cambridge: Cambridge University Press.

Majumdar, R.C. 1961. Ideas of History in Sanskrit Literature. In C.H. Philips (ed.). *Historians of India, Pakistan and Ceylon,* pp. 13-28. London: Oxford University Press.

Paddayya, K. 1990. *The New Archaeology and Aftermath: A View from Outside the Anglo-American World.* Pune: Ravish Publishers.

——. 1993. C.J. Thomsen and Three Age System. *Man and Environment* 18: 129-40.

——. 1994. Sir William Jones: The Father of Oriental Research. *University News* (May 23, 1994): 15-17.

——. 1996. Sir William Jones: A Tribute. *Bulletin of the Deccan College Research Institute.* 54-55 (1994-95): xv-xxxv.

——. 2002. Ancient Indian Thought: A Component of Liberal Education. *University News.* (31 December 2001-6 January 2002): 3-9.

——. 2012. On Nehru's Concept of Scientific Temper of Mind and its Place in Modern India. *Propagation* 3(1): 23-26.

Petrie, W.M. Flinders. 1972. *Methods and Aims in Archaeology.* New York: Benjamin Blom, Inc. Originally published in 1904.

Sabloff, Jeremy A. 2008. *Archaeology Matters: Action Archaeology in the Modern World.* Walnut Creek, California: Left Coast Press.

Sankalia, H.D. 1965. Archaeology and Education. In V.N. Misra and M.S. Mate (eds.), *Indian Prehistory: 1964,* 257-62. Pune: Deccan College.

Sen, A. 1993 India and the West. *New Republic* 208: 27-35.

——. 1996a. *On Interpreting India's Past.* Kolkata: The Asiatic Society.

——. 1996b. Taking Pride in a Pluralistic Society. *Span* (June-July 1996): 8-23.

——. 1999a. *Development as Freedom*. New Delhi: Oxford University Press.

——. 1999b. Capability and Well-being. In M.C. Nussbaum and A. Sen (ed.), *The Quality of Life*, pp.30-53. New Delhi: Oxford University Press.

Singh, Baldev. 1986. *Jawaharlal Nehru on Science*. New Delhi: Nehru Memorial Museum and Library.

Smith, Steven G. 2009. Historical Meaningfulness in Shared Action. *History and Theory* 48: 1-19.

Southgate, B. 1996. *History: What and Why? Ancient, Modern and Postmodern Perspectives.* London: Routledge.

——. 2000. *Why Bother with History? Ancient, Modern, and Postmodern Motivations.* Harlow (U.K.): Pearson Education.

Index